D1732877

Terry Texas Ranger Trilogy

Benjamin Franklin Terry was the organizer and first colonel of the Rangers. Earlier he had gone to Virginia and was a staff officer at the first battle of Manassas. He was killed in a skirmish at Woodsonville, Kentucky, 17 December 1861. Terry County in Texas was named in his honor.

Plate 1

Terry Texas Ranger Trilogy

Terry's Texas Rangers
by L.B. Giles

Reminiscences of the Terry Rangers
by J.K.P. Blackburn

The Diary of Ephraim Shelby Dodd
by E.S. Dodd

Introduction by Thomas W. Cutrer

State House Press
Austin, Texas
1996

Library of Congress Cataloging-in-Publication Data

Terry Texas Ranger trilogy / [edited with an] introduction
by Thomas W. Cutrer.
p.   cm.
Includes index.
Contents: Terry Texas Rangers / by L. B. Giles —
Reminiscences of the Terry Rangers / by J.K.P. Blackburn
— The Diary of Ephraim Shelby Dodd / by E.S. Dodd.
ISBN 1-880510-45-6 (alk. paper).
ISBN 1-880510-46-4 (pbk. : alk. paper)
ISBN 1-880510-47-2 (ltd. : (alk. paper)
1. Confederate States of America. Army. Texas Cavalry
Regiment, 8th. 2. Texas—History—Civil War,
1861-1865—Regimental histories. 3. United
States—History—Civil War, 1861-1865—Regimental
histories. 4. United States—History—Civil War,
1861-1865—Personal narratives, Confederate. I. Giles,
L.B. Terry Texas Rangers. II. Blackburn, J.K.P.
Reminiscenes of the Terry Rangers. III. Dodd, E.S.
(Ephraim Shelby Dodd). The Diary of Ephraim Shelby
Dodd. IV. Cutrer, Thomas W.

E580.6 8th.T47 1996
973.7'464—dc20   96-22469

Printed in the United States of America

cover design by David Timmons

COVER ILLUSTRATION:
"C.S.A. 8th Cavalry Terry's Texas Rangers" from a
painting by Raymond Desvarreux Larpenteur.
© Alfred B.C. Batson & David R. Vanderslice.
10-1/2" x 16" prints can be ordered from
Red's Military Prints, P.O. Box 1071, Ringgold, GA 30736

STATE HOUSE PRESS
P.O. Box 15247
Austin, Texas 78761

Table of Contents

Introduction

A Union officer, whose misfortune it had been to cross swords with the Eighth Texas Cavalry, observed that "the Texas Rangers are as quick as lightening. They ride like Arabs, shoot like archers at a mark, and fight like devils." One of the most colorful and effective units in American military history, the Eighth Texas Cavalry, better known as Terry's Texas Rangers, was among the most famous regiments, North and South, to serve in the American Civil War. "The career of this regiment," wrote Brig. Gen. Thomas Jordan, who had ample opportunity to observe the unit while serving as Albert Sidney Johnston's adjutant general and as chief of staff to both P. G. T. Beauregard and Braxton Bragg, "has been one of the most brilliant in the annals of war."

This elite unit was the creation of Benjamin Franklin Terry, a wealthy Fort Bend County sugar planter. After distinguishing himself as a volunteer aide at the first battle of Manassas, Terry sought and received authorization from the Confederate War Department to raise a regiment of cavalry for service in Virginia, and on 12 August 1861 he issued a call for volunteers. Each man was required to furnish his own arms and equipment, a shotgun or carbine, at least one Colt revolver, a Bowie knife, and a saddle, bridle, and blanket. The army would provide the regiment with mounts.

Although Benjamin Franklin Burke of Company F admitted that "We have got a good many rowdys in our company," the personnel of the Terry Rangers was generally "of the highest order," drawn from the best families in Central and South Texas. Brig. Gen. Thomas Jordan, a West Point-trained Virginian, concurred, observing that the rank-and-file of the Rangers included "a number of the wealthiest and best educated young men of Texas." Many were college graduates, professional men, merchants, stockmen and planters; all were young, in their teens and early twenties, and each man wore his pistols "as regularly as clothes."

Terry's was a democratic regiment in a democratic army. "Rank was not considered and when tendered, refused," Burke commented, and Pvt. Henry W. Graber of Company B agreed that "a private was generally the equal of any officer in command." If rank counted for little, discipline counted for less. Pvt. L. B. Giles admitted that "from the standpoint of the martinet our organization could scarcely be called a regiment." Indeed, "if there was ever any serious attempt to discipline it the effort was soon abandoned. Volunteers we began, volunteers we remained to the end." But to the credit of the Rangers, he added, "few ever avoided a fight." Albert Sidney Johnston agreed. "With a little more drill," he told them, "you are the equals of the Old Guard of Napoleon."

What was important to the men was that they serve in the cavalry. "I would rather be corporal in Company 'F' of the Texas Rangers than first Lieu in a flatfoot company," wrote Corp. John Wesley Rabb. General Jordan noted that the men of the Eighth Texas Cavalry, "specially trained in the business of stock raising on the vast prairies of that state, had acquired a marvelous skill in horsemanship," and as Lt.-Col. James Arthur Lyon Fremantle of Her Majesty's

Coldstream Guards observed, "At the outbreak of the war it was found very difficult to raise infantry in Texas, as no Texan walks a yard if he can help it." Governor Edward Clark, too, noted "the predilection of Texans for cavalry service." This penchant, he told the state legislature, "founded as it is upon their peerless horsemanship, is so powerful that they are unwilling in many instances to engage in service of any other description."

Robert Franklin Bunting, the Rangers' Pennsylvania-born chaplain, stated the case even more forcefully. "It is a burning shame," he wrote, "that such horsemen as Texians are, and I may justly add, such fighters, too, should be put in the infantry service." Cavalrymen from other states, "poorly mounted, poorly armed, and shamefully poor horse-men," he considered a reproach to "the honorable arm of the service, and . . . a loss to the web foots where they would be compelled to do good fighting." More ardently even than the rest of their fellow Southerners, Texans saw themselves as the heirs of the knightly tradition and the sons of the cavaliers of old England. Graber was to observe that "the average cavalryman feels near half whipped if he has to leave his horse any great distance, to fight." A man on foot was but half a man.

Graber explained the regiment's remarkable élan this way: "we started out with the name of 'Texas Rangers,' with a reputation we had never earned but were called on to sustain." Texas Rangers had served with great distinction against Indians and Mexicans during the period of the Republic and had gained an international reputation during the United States' war with Mexico, 1846-1848. The name Texas Ranger was never to be taken lightly, and although officially only another Texas cavalry regiment, Terry's men no doubt felt it their special duty to uphold the honor of the old Rangers now, beyond the Mississippi. The *Houston Telegraph* predicted that the "regiment will be the pride of

Texas," for its troopers "will feel they have an ancient and glorious fame to sustain. We hazard nothing in saying that there is an amount of manliness, chivalry, and bravery in the regiment, which cannot be surpassed by any troops in the world."

Having mustered in at Houston on 19 September 1861, and swearing to serve "so far as the war shall last," the regiment, officially designated the Eighth Texas Cavalry but more popularly known as Terry's Texas Rangers, or more simply the Terry Rangers and informally as the "Terry-fiers" and "Terry's Terribles," set out for the war. The first leg of their journey, from Houston to Beaumont, was made by rail and horseback; Lake Charles, Louisiana, was reached by steamboat; the next one hundred miles to New Iberia was waded. The swamp water was waist deep in a great many places, Private Burke wrote to his mother. "It was very fortunate that we got horses or we would have had an awfull [sic] time of it, although we had about as bad a time as I ever wish to have again." Finally, once again water borne, the weary regiment reached New Orleans on 30 September. There they received orders from Gen. Albert Sidney Johnston, commander of all Confederate forces west of the Appalachian Mountains, to join him and his command at Bowling Green, Kentucky.

Although the men were vociferously disappointed at being reassigned from the pivotal fighting in Virginia, they were somewhat mollified by the promise of service under a fellow Texan personally known to many of them, and by Johnston's promise that they would be mounted on "the best horses that Kentucky afforded and that we should always remain a separate and distinct command, never to be brigaded with any other troops as long as he lived." Johnston, formerly a brigadier general in the Army of the Republic of Texas, was well acquainted with the character of Texans, regarding them, in Graber's words, as "a fearless and enthusiastic people, proud of their Texas history; and, knowing the young men composing this regiment would endeavor to emulate the example of the heroes of the Alamo, Goliad and San Jacinto."

In response to their requisition of tents and cooking utensils at New Orleans, Maj. Gen. David Twiggs, formerly the United States commander of the Department of Texas but now Confederate commander of the District of Louisiana replied, "Who ever heard of a Texas Ranger carrying cooking utensils and sleeping in a tent?" and sent them on to Tennessee with neither. Suffering a further affront to their comfort, the Rangers rode to the war in box cars that had been used for shipping cattle and which, according to Giles, "were not overly clean." Seats were rough, backless planks, and "in this luxurious fashion" the regiment rode for twenty hours to Nashville.

There they encamped on the Fair Grounds, which Private Burke called "the most beatiful [sic] place for a soldier camp I ever saw." The Texans were treated as celebrities, glorying in exhibitions of their horsemanship and marksmanship for the local population. The Rangers, wrote Giles, were the first "'wild-west' entertainment ever seen east of the Mississippi," and the men earned the admiration of the people of Nashville, and some pocket money as well, by picking silver dollars from the ground at a dead gallop. In all, the Texans were treated with great hospitality and respect in "the great city of Nashvill [sic]" but, wrote Burke, "I would[n't] give Texas for all of it."

From Nashville the regiment reported to Johnston's headquarters at Bowling Green, Kentucky, where they drew their horses, tents, and camp utensils and completed their regimental organization by formally electing Terry as their colonel, Thomas S. Lubbock as their lieutenant colonel, and Thomas Harrison as their major.

Terry, a native of Kentucky, was forty years old and,

according to Giles, "of great force of character, firm and self-reliant. His appearance was commanding and in all ways he was fitted for high rank." Lubbock, forty-four years old and in ill health, was a native of South Carolina. "Small of stature, pleasant and affable," according to Giles, he "made a favorable impression" on the men. Harrison was a native of Mississippi, a lawyer by profession, small, nervous, and irascible, but he proved to be a fine soldier and became a brigadier general in the final months of the war.

At Bowling Green the Texans also began to learn the art and science of soldiering, and were introduced to close order drill and "Hardee's Tactics." Although the Rangers did not take well to formal military discipline, even Benjamin Burke was impressed by the pomp and circumstance of a well regulated camp of instruction. "Things around here look somewhat like war to see that many troops drilling and the music going on continually," he wrote.

From their winter quarters at Ritters, Kentucky, the regiment screened the army, their tireless vigilance causing Lt. Gen. William J. Hardee to remark, "I always feel safe when the Rangers are in front." Scouting and picket duty in the unaccustomed snow and freezing rain, however, took their toll. Pneumonia and measles struck the Rangers hard, sending more than six hundred to the hospitals, home on convalescent leave or invalided, or to a premature grave. After only one month at Ritters, Graber counted only "about 400 for duty," and Blackburn estimated that "as many or perhaps more in our regiment died in this epidemic than were killed in battle." Yet the Rangers were "tolerably well attended to" according to Burke, "there being plenty of lady nurses in the hospital."

Eager for "an enterprize [sic] among the enemy," the Rangers were pleased to join Brig. Gen. Thomas C. Hindman's infantry brigade and artillery battery in seeking, contrary to Johnston's expressed wishes, a confrontation with the enemy. On 8 December Hindman pushed his command, with Terry's men in the vanguard, up toward the Union camps on Green River near Woodsonville. Just below Rowlett Station the Rangers encountered a line of enemy infantry and, in Burke's words, "thought we would devil them some before we left them." Hindman, now inclined toward caution, ordered the Texans back to await the infantry and field guns, but it was now Terry's turn to disregard orders and take more aggressive action. Not being one "to invite visitors and then leave someone else to entertain them," Terry informed Hindman that "this is no place for you; go back to your infantry," and ordered his regiment to form into line and charge.

Col. August von Willich, commander of the Thirty-second Indiana Infantry, recalled how "With lightning speed, under infernal yelling, great numbers of Texas Rangers rushed upon our whole force. They advanced to fifteen or twenty yards of our lines, some of them even between them, and opened fire with rifles and revolvers." The shock of galloping horses and shotgun and revolver fire pouring in at close range broke the Union line and sent the men streaming to the rear in panic.

This was the first engagement of what was to become the Army of Tennessee, the principal Confederate army in the West. Not atypically, it resulted in a Confederate victory achieved with much élan and gallantry but bought at too high a price. Among those slain on this otherwise unimportant field was Col. Benjamin Franklin Terry. His loss was mourned throughout the Confederacy, and Graber speculated that, "considering his fearlessness and dash, as also his ability as a commander, he would have proved another Forrest, a Napoleon of cavalry."

Lubbock advanced to the command of the regiment, and John G. Walker became its lieutenant colonel. When Lubbock died within a few days of his promotion, Capt. John A.

Wharton of Company B was chosen to fill his place. "Wharton was a man of ability, of a distinguished family, liberally educated, a lawyer and a captivating public speaker," Giles recalled. "Enterprising and ambitious, he never forgot during the wakeful moment that the soldier who survived the war would be a voter." By the time of the battle of Shiloh, Wharton commanded the regiment. In November 1862 he advanced to the rank of brigadier general and to major general in November 1863. General Wharton was transferred to the Trans-Mississippi theater in the spring of 1864, following the death of Maj. Gen. Thomas Green at the battle of Blair's Landing, and was given command of the cavalry in Lt. Gen. Richard Taylor's district. On 6 April 1865 Col. George W. Baylor assassinated Wharton in Houston in a quarrel over "military matters."

Albert Sidney Johnston's "Tennessee Line," perforated as it was by numerous navigable waterways but boasting hardly a mile of naturally defensible terrain, was soon severed by Union columns supported by gunboats moving up the Cumberland and Tennessee rivers. The Army of Tennessee was forced to evacuate Kentucky and northern Tennessee when Fort Donelson and Fort Henry fell in February 1862. The Rangers covered the army's retreat from Bowling Green, through Nashville, and on into northern Mississippi. In all, the army fell back 350 miles over bad roads with little food for the men or forage or grain for the horses. "I reckon you will be very much surprised when you hear of our long retreat and evacuation of Kentucky and Tennessee," Burke wrote to his father. "It has astonished me very much that we should take such a move and even without having any fighting. When it is all sumed [sic] up the truth is that we have been out generalled by the North."

Halting the retreat at Corinth, Mississippi, however, Johnston planned the counterstroke which he hoped would win back all of lost Tennessee and Kentucky for the South.

With Maj. Gen. Ulysses S. Grant's army camped unawares at Pittsburg Landing on the Tennessee River, and the army of Maj. Gen. Don Carlos Buell still a day's march away, Johnston planned a swift surprise attack to throw Grant into the Tennessee before Buell could come to his assistance. On the march from Corinth to Pittsburg Landing, the Terry Rangers covered the left wing of the Confederate army. "In detachments," wrote Blackburn, "we guarded every road, trail and opening around the whole left front and flank."

On Sunday, 6 April 1862, the Confederate army overran the Federal camps around Shiloh Church and drove the astounded enemy almost at will to the banks of the Tennessee. "We found any amount of camp equipage of every description," wrote the awed Burke, "and more provisions and clothing than you could shake a stick at." The Rebels marveled at the copious quantities of luxury items which they found in the Federal tents. Especially intriguing was the variety of exotic foods from the suttler's stores. The hungry Texans found "most anything you could mention almost to eat, such as hams, sugar, crackers, amons [sic], candy, oysters, sardines, etc., etc., and also fine segars [sic] and chewing tobacco." The Rangers saw but limited service at Shiloh, however, being unable to fight on horseback in the tangled undergrowth and of only limited effectiveness when fighting on foot armed with shotguns against the Union's Springfield rifles.

Late in the afternoon of 6 April, Albert Sidney Johnston received a fatal wound and died on the field. "This we then regarded as a calamity," wrote Ranger Giles, "and time has not changed our opinion." With Johnston's death, Gen. Pierre G. T. Beauregard assumed command and, believing that Grant's army was crushed and required only to be marched away to Southern prison camps, ordered his troops to halt their attacks and regroup for the next day's final assault. During the night, however, Buell's fresh column crossed the Tennessee and rallied Grant's shattered and demoralized men. With the two Union forces united, Beauregard saw the inevitability of a Southern disaster if the fight were continued and began to extricate his decimated regiments. The second day of the battle of Shiloh was characterized by the stubborn retreat of the Southern army through the Federal camps captured on the previous day.

On the morning of 8 April, the third day of the battle, Beauregard called upon Brig. Gen. John C. Breckenridge and his infantry brigade, Col. Nathan Bedford Forrest and fifty of his troopers, and the Eighth Texas Cavalry to serve as the rear guard while the Rebel army began the painful withdrawal toward Corinth. Here the regiment was in its element, for as Lt. Gen. Braxton Bragg commented, "There is no danger of a surprise when the Rangers are between us and the enemy."

Near the edge of the battlefield the rear guard found itself confronted by a brigade of Federal cavalry supported by a double line of infantry prepared to overtake the rear of the retreating column and once again bring on a general engage-ment, one in which the Confederates could not hope to compete. Defying the odds, the Texans under Major Harri-son, their last unwounded field grade officer, and Forrest's tiny escort charged the Federal vanguard. "Boys, go in twenty steps of the Yankees before you turn your shotguns loose on them," ordered Harrison. The desperate attack broke both the Union's cavalry and infantry lines and checked further pursuit of Beauregard's crippled army.

B. F. Burke described the scene in a letter to his father: "On tuesday [sic] after all our inphantry [sic] had fallen back some distance from the battle ground all of the cavalry was thrown in the rear. Well about twelve o'clock in the day some of our cavalry spied some of the Yankee cavalry who were pursuing us, so they turned on them and put them all to flight. Their numbers was about 15 hundred cavalry and about one thousand inphantry. Our Texas boys were the principle [sic] ones in the fight." This dare-devil charge was the last action on the field of Shiloh and one of the most tactically decisive, saving the Southern army from further harassment and possible annihilation at the hands of the fresh and more numerous Union forces.

According to Blackburn, of the sixty-five men and two officers of Company F who answered roll call on the morning of 6 April, only the captain and fourteen men were present for duty by the battle's end. A total of sixty-five Rangers were killed or wounded in "the great battle of Shiloh," which Burke characterized as "the most awfull [sic] battle I ever expect to hear or see."

After Shiloh and Johnston's death, Beauregard brigaded the Rangers with a Kentucky regiment under Col. John Adams and ordered them on a raid into middle Tennessee. They crossed the Tennessee River at Lamb's Ferry, where they left their camp equipage, the last wagons, extra luggage or cooking utensils the Texans were ever to have for Federal cavalry to capture.

Adams proceeded with too much caution for the Rangers' tastes, passing opportunities for fighting and plunder. "We were chased by the Yankees pretty near all the time we were over there," complained Burke. "They were over in [enemy] country about 3 weeks and never had but one little fight. About a hundred of our regiment and Kentuckians got drunk one day and ran into the town [of] Winchester and ran about a thousand Yankees out. . . . That's all the engagement they had while out." When Adams ordered a withdrawal to Chattanooga to procure a battery of artillery, stating that he "would not undertake to remain in middle Tennessee without it," Wharton rebelled, declaring that he and his regiment would remain in middle Tennessee and follow Beauregard's order and Adams could "go to Halifax."

Maj. Gen. Edmund Kirby Smith, commander of the

District of East Tennessee, ordered the Eighth Texas Cavalry to report at McMinnville to Forrest, now the commander of the cavalry brigade of the Army of Tennessee. "Under his leadership," said the admiring Giles, "our metal was not to grow rusty." On 8 July the Rangers, with Forrest's Fourth Tennessee Cavalry and First and Second Georgia Cavalry regiments, started toward the headquarters of Union Brig. Gen. Thomas Turpin Crittenden at Murfreesboro, Tennessee. Arriving on 13 July, Forrest immediately launched a surprise attack on the large Union garrison, charging through the town and enemy camps.

Employing an outrageous ruse and cold-blooded bluff, "If you refuse I will charge you with the Texas Rangers under the black flag" he told the Federals, Forrest induced 1,040 of the enemy to surrender and to give up four pieces of artillery and a mountain of commissary and quartermaster stores. General Crittenden himself was found hiding in the tavern. In the words of D. S. Combs, a private in Company D, Forrest just "swooped down on the two camps and took them in out of the damp." The Rangers "now felt like they were commanded by somebody who meant business," Graber wrote, and Burke reported to his father that "the boys are all in high spirits thinking we will soon be in possession of the entire state of Tennessee."

The raid continued to Nashville where Forrest made a demonstration against the city's impregnable defenses before contenting himself with capturing Union mail and troop trains and destroying track and trestles. After the sensationally successful Tennessee raid, the Rangers were ordered back to Chattanooga for scouting and picketing duty. There they sparred with Federal cavalry patrols, parried an occasional thrust of infantry and artillery columns, and once even did battle with a Federal gunboat that had run downstream to harass the city.

In September 1862 the Terry Rangers once again entered

middle Tennessee in support of Gen. Braxton Bragg, now in command of the Army of Tennessee, for his invasion of Kentucky. Forrest's brigade, under the temporary command of Colonel Wharton, cut to the northeast, intercepting the army's line of march at Bardstown, Kentucky, and awaited Bragg's arrival. There, on 4 October 1862, was fought what Graber described as "one of the most brilliant cavalry engagements we were in." The Confederate cavalry's successful defense of Bardstown, "one of the softest snaps in the way of a fight that we had during the war," according to Giles, held open the route north for Bragg's infantry and earned Wharton a promotion to the rank of brigadier general.

With the arrival of the main army, Forrest's brigade was added to Col. Joseph Wheeler's cavalry division and served as part of the rear guard as the Army of Tennessee drove further north into Kentucky.

Although they were able to hold the pursuing Federals at bay for a few days while Bragg's infantry accumulated recruits and supplies, the enemy was able to bring on a general engagement at Perryville on 8 October 1862. In this, the largest battle ever fought on Kentucky soil, the Rangers occupied the extreme right of the Rebel line and "did a full share of the fighting." Early in the afternoon the Rangers made a mounted charge across the creek which separated the two armies, "up the hill and into the woods among the Yankees. This whole movement was made at a sweeping gallop and as if on parade," remembered Pvt. A. B. Briscoe of Company D. "How different from the way we were handled at Shiloh!" Replaced in the line of battle by infantry troops, the Eighth Texas went looking for a fight on the enemy's left and rear but found the approaches to the Federal supply train too closely guarded to attack successfully.

Although the battle was technically a draw, Bragg began a retreat southward from Perryville that night with the cavalry once more serving as rear guard. "We had a pretty tight time of it," said Burke. "We had a fight every day with them and had to stand under fire of their cannon, though lost but very few men. Our reg't done the greatest portion of the picketing." Worse, the Rebel horsemen concluded the Kentucky campaign with decidedly empty bellies and haversacks. The Rangers were too occupied with keeping the Yankees away from the rear elements of the army to forage, complained Blackburn, and so "fasted and fought for days without anything worth mentioning."

Buell's Federals pursued Bragg's retreating army for a week until the Rebels were able to take a strong defensive position at Cumberland Gap. There, on 23 October 1862, General Wheeler commended his cavalry for having been scarcely out of musket range of the enemy for nearly two months during the Kentucky campaign. Wheeler counted more than twenty pitched battles and some one hundred skirmishes in which his troopers had engaged a more numerous enemy. "Your continuous contact with the enemy has taught you to repose without fear under his guns," he told them, "to fight wherever he is found, and to make your bivouac by the light of his camp fires."

From Cumberland Gap the army moved again into middle Tennessee, establishing its headquarters beside Stones River at Murfreesboro, where Thomas Harrison replaced Wharton as commander of the regiment and Wharton took command of Forrest's old brigade. "The weather is getting pretty cold up here now," Burke informed his parents, "and blankets and bed clothing is very scarcer [sic] & also clothing of all kinds." The regiment spent its second Christmas, Giles recalled, "a serious and sober set, thinking of the homes and loved ones far away, and wondering if we should ever see them again."

From 31 December 1862 through 2 January 1863 the Confederate Army of Tennessee fought the Union Army of the Cumberland to another bloody stalemate at Murfreesboro. Graber was satisfied that the Ranger regiment had "fully sustained their character as one of the leading regiments in this army, capturing prisoners, artillery, wagon trains, etc., and finally covering the retreat of the army off the field." The Rangers were "not found idle during the day," agreed Burke. "They were busily engaged in cha[r]ging the flanks of the enemy & also in charging upon the wagon train of the enemy." The Rangers captured a battery of Union artillery during the first day's fighting, and on the thirty-first Wheeler's cavalry attacked the enemy's rear, capturing and burning a Union supply train of thirty wagons. On the fourth day, to the great surprise of the Texans, Bragg retreated.

The outnumbered Bragg felt that he had not the resources to destroy or drive the enemy from the field, and apparently thought best that he should withdraw his army to reorganize and recover from the three-day blood-letting. The army, however, once again felt betrayed by its high command. "I don't know what he [Bragg] ever left Murfreesboro for," complained an increasingly disillusioned Burke. "For he had them badly whipped when he left there." Giles, too, had developed a hearty distrust of General Bragg. "The only tactics he seems to have learned," he wrote, "was to wait till the enemy came up to his lines and fortified himself; then attack and lose more men than the enemy, then sneak away." Bragg retreated through Shelbyville and Tullahoma, opening for the Union army the route to the strategically vital city of Chattanooga.

In January 1863 the Confederate cavalry reentered Tennessee on yet another raid. "Just who conceived this wild-goose chase, I am not informed. For sufferings, hardships, and barrenness of results, it is only exceeded by Napoleon's Russian campaign," Giles complained. The weather was brutally cold, and according to the semi-literate but keenly observant Burke, the route was "the roughest road to travail [*sic*] that ever men travailed."

On 20 September 1863, after rejoining Bragg's army in northwest Georgia, the Rangers took part in the battle of Chickamauga. "It was such dearly fought and fruitless victories as this which finally defeated the South," Giles believed. The defeat at Gettysburg, the fall of Vicksburg, and the evacuation of Tennessee "cast quite [a] gloom over our future," Burke agreed, although he and his comrades still had faith in an ultimate Confederate victory.

In November 1863 the Eighth Texas Cavalry was again detached from the Army of Tennessee, then besieging Chattanooga, and followed Lt. Gen. James Longstreet's corps into east Tennessee as part of Maj. Gen. William T. Martin's cavalry division. There they took part in the fruitless siege of Knoxville from 17 November through 4 December. Braxton Bragg's defeat at Chattanooga, 24-25 November 1863, forced Longstreet to raise his siege and fall back into northern Georgia and sent Confederate public morale spiraling downward.

Burke wrote to his mother and father that although many civilians were becoming "somewhat despondent," he did not believe the army was much demoralized. "We have met with reverses of late that has almost been enough to make us despondent especially Texans and Tennesseeans. We are now entirely cut off from our homes and cannot even have the pleasure of hearing from them. But notwithstanding all these circumstances and the many dark clouds that are now hovering around us, I believe we will come out victorious at last."

In March 1864 the Terry Rangers rejoined the Army of Tennessee at Dalton, Georgia. There its new commander, Gen. Joseph E. Johnston, was preparing to begin the spring campaign to defend Atlanta. Despite their joy at being rid of Bragg, the aggressive Texas regiment was less than favorably impressed by Johnston's delaying actions against Maj.

Gen. William T. Sherman's Federals between Rocky Face Ridge, 5-11 May, and the Chattahoochie River, 4-9 July 1864. For a while they were dismounted and introduced to the pick and shovel. Graber bitterly complained of being turned into "an army of laborers by day and travelers by night."

In the action around Atlanta, however, the Rangers were again called into mounted service, facing Maj. Gen. George Stoneman, chief of cavalry in Maj. Gen. John M. Schofield's Army of the Ohio. During the last week of July, Stoneman "undertook to play our game," as Giles wrote, sending two columns of cavalry raiding deep behind Rebel lines. The Southern cavalry, always contemptuous of the mounted arm of the Federal army, soundly whipped both of these parties on the Chattahoochie River near Macon, taking more than fifteen hundred prisoners including Stoneman himself.

After the repulse of Stoneman's raid, Wheeler's cavalry was ordered to operate on the long line of Sherman's communications, hoping to divert the Federal army's attention from Atlanta, and so slipped back into Tennessee, interdicting the enemy's rail connections with the North. Sherman merely cut loose from his line of supply and ordered his army to live off the land. "It did not take one with much intellect to see that one of the greatest cavalry raids of the war was a failure," said Graber.

Following the fall of Atlanta on 1 September 1864, the Rebel cavalry covered the march of Gen. John Bell Hood, who had superseded Johnston as commander of the Army of Tennessee, on his move to the Tennessee River, once more in hopes of turning Sherman's attention from Georgia and pulling him back into Tennessee. After some heavy skirmishing around Rome, Georgia, where the Terry Rangers lost their battle flag at the "Rome Races," the cavalry returned to Sherman's front below Atlanta, arriving on 9 October 1864, while "the gallant Hood of Texas" launched off into Tennessee on his march toward disastrous defeat at the hands of Schofield and Maj. Gen. George H. Thomas at the battles of Franklin and Nashville.

Wheeler's cavalry was almost the only obstacle in Sherman's path to the sea. "Times looked rather gloomy at this time," Burke wrote. "It seems like the Yankees are sending innumerable hords [sic] against us on evry [sic] side but not so much yet but what we give them a decent flogging once and a while. Provisions and forage is getting pretty scarce here, though we are not suffering as yet if it don't get any worse."

As Sherman ploughed his sixty-mile-wide swath through Georgia, Wheeler's troopers grimly harried his front, contesting every inch of the route through Macon to Savannah and the sea with Brig. Gen. Judson Kilpatrick's Yankee cavalry. "Our service," wrote Graber, "was to keep his cavalry from foraging, burning, and destroying the country." Bitter delaying actions were fought at Buck Head Creek, Griswoldville and Waynesborough but, desperately outnumbered, the Southern horsemen could offer but little resistance, and in daily fighting their losses were heavy. By the time the regiment entered North Carolina, the Eighth Texas Cavalry had lost every one of its field grade officers and was commanded by a captain.

At last, at Bentonville, on 19-20 March 1865, Johnston staged the *Götterdämmerung* of the Army of Tennessee. There the Terry Rangers executed "one of the most brilliant charges ever made by cavalry," securing the army's route of retreat, the Mill Creek bridge on the Confederate rear. The bridge was guarded by some of Maj. Gen. Wade Hampton's South Carolina cavalry when Sherman ordered elements of Maj. Gen. Joseph Anthony Mower's XX Corps to make a dash around the Rebel left to capture and destroy it, thus trapping the remnant of the once-proud Army of Tennessee.

When Mower easily dispersed Hampton's men, William J.

Hardee dashed up to what remained of the Eighth Texas Cavalry—some two hundred men—and asked "Who commands this regiment?" He was answered by Capt. J. F. "Doc" Matthews of Company K, the senior officer present for duty. "Can you hold those people in check until I can bring up the infantry and artillery?" Hardee demanded. "Gen., we are the boys that can try," Matthews responded, and called to the Rangers, "Come on!"

Although Giles thought that "It looked like the old regiment was this time surely going to its grave," the Texans raised "their accustomed yell and with their pistols, dashed into the first line of infantry." Almost miraculously, the Federal advance was thrown into confusion and sent streaming to the rear. The Rangers withdrew with a number of prisoners, and Hardee quickly brought up infantry and artillery to hold the bridge until night when the army crossed to safety. The Terry Rangers had thus delivered the first charge of the Army of Tennessee and its last.

On 25 April 1865, the night before the surrender of Johnston's army, the regiment was camped at Smithfield, North Carolina. Although reduced to "little more than a good company," the Rangers still had no intention of giving up. Even when General Wheeler personally advised them to accept parole, the greater part of them demurred. "You have fought your fight," Wheeler told them. "Your task is done. During a four year's struggle for liberty you have exhibited courage, fortitude, and devotion. You are the victors of more than 200 sternly contested fields. You have participated in more than a thousand conflicts of arms. . . . You have done all that human exertion could accomplish." Under the terms of the surrender cavalry would be allowed to retain their horses and side arms and go home with parole; otherwise, if caught they would be shot as guerrillas. Still, when General Harrison, who had been wounded and left behind some weeks earlier, called the Rangers to him, they came.

Graber, for one, believed that the whole army would be incarcerated, and had "determined never to see the inside of another prison."

Capt. J. F. Matthews, the last commander of the Eighth Texas Cavalry, surrendered only ninety of the 248 Rangers reported to have been in camp the night before the surrender. The rest made their way out and reported to Harrison, intent upon continuing the fight under Lt. Gen. Richard Taylor at Mobile or to help sustain Kirby Smith's forlorn hope of perpetuating the Confederate government beyond the Mississippi.

Across South Carolina and Georgia they skirmished with bushwhackers and such Yankee cavalry as they could not avoid, subsisting on enemy stores and capturing enemy mules where possible. In route they heard of the flight of President Davis and his cabinet, the surrender of Taylor's small command, and the assassination of Abraham Lincoln; but worse news awaited them in Alabama. There the fugitives learned that the Mississippi River was flooding out of its banks, too wide to ford or ferry, and were told that Kirby Smith had surrendered the last Rebels under arms. Most of the remaining Rangers therefore abandoned their attempt to reach Shreveport and determined to get to Texas as best they could.

Ironically, only after the disorganized Rangers arrived by ones and twos in Louisiana did Kirby Smith lay down his arms; the earlier report of his surrender, which had been current in Alabama, had been only a rumor. Thus the last of the Eighth Texas Cavalry returned home to "a sad, dejected and ruined people, resolved," as Graber wrote, "to do the best they could under the circumstances and submit gracefully to the powers that were."

The best-known testaments to the Rangers' remarkable Civil War career are the memoirs of J. K. P. Blackburn and L. B. Giles and the personal diary of E. P. Dodd. Together these documents constitute not only the finest primary source materials relating to this extraordinary regiment, but also tell a vastly entertaining tale of courage, loyalty and high adventure.[*]

James Knox Polk Blackburn was born in Maury County, Tennessee, on 20 February 1837 and emigrated to Fayette County, Texas, in fall of 1856. He attended the Alma Male and Female Institute in Halletsville, the seat of Lavaca County, and upon graduation taught school in Fayette, Gonzales, and Lavaca counties. In Lavaca at the time of Texas' secession, Blackburn first joined Capt. Frederick J. Malone's local militia company, to which he was elected first lieutenant. In that capacity he served with the legendary Ben McCulloch at the capture of San Antonio on 16 February 1861.

In September 1861, however, upon learning that the Terry Rangers were enlisting recruits in Fayette County, he is said to have walked the 110 miles to LaGrange to volunteer. With the regiment's organization, Blackburn was elected first lieutenant of Capt. Louis M. Strobel's Company F, and was later promoted to captain and company commander. Blackburn was seriously wounded in both thighs at Farmington, Mississippi, 7 October 1863, and captured by the enemy. He recuperated in Giles County, Tennessee,

---

* For additional published letters and memoirs by Terry Rangers, the reader may consult Henry W. Graber, *The Life Record of of H.W. Graber, A Terry Texas Ranger*, 1861-1865 (Dallas: privately published, 1916; reprint, Austin: State House Press, 1987, as *A Terry Texas Ranger*, with introduction by Thomas W. Cutrer; William Andrew Fletcher, *Rebel Private, Front and Rear* (Beaumont: Greet Print, 1908; reprint, Austin: University of Texas Press, 1954, with introduction by Bell I. Wiley); Ralph A. Wooster and Roger W. Williams, Jr., eds., "With Terry's Texas Rangers, the Letters of Issac Dunbar Afflick," *Civil War History*. IX, (1963), 299-319; Helen J. H. Rugeley, ed., *Batchelor-Turner Letters*, 1861-1864 (Austin: Steck Co., 1961); and Thomas W. Cutrer, ed. "'We Are Stern and Resolved': The Civil War Letters of John Wesley Rabb, Terry's Texas Rangers," *Southwestern Historical Quarterly*, XCI, (1987), 185-226.

and after recovery and parole, returned to his regiment in February 1865, almost too late to surrender with the remnants of the Army of Tennessee at Durham Station, North Carolina.

Rather than return to Texas, Blackburn settled in Giles County after the war, where he became a planter and, later, a member of the Tennessee state legislature. There too, on 10 February 1867, he married Mary McMillan Laird. At the urging of his family and friends, Blackburn also began to write his recollections of his days with the Terry Rangers, finishing the book at Lynnville, Tennessee, in 1916. His niece, Mrs. W. D. Hunter of Austin, transcribed the manuscript and returned with her copy to Texas where it came to the attention of Professor Charles W. Ramsdell of the University of Texas. Ramsdell edited Blackburn's memoir for publication in the *Southwestern Historical Quarterly* in 1918 and 1919 as *Reminiscences of the Terry Texas Rangers*. It was first reprinted in a soft-cover edition in 1919 by the University of Texas Littlefield Fund for Southern History, subsidized by the successful cattle rancher George Washington Littlefield, himself a former major in the Terry Rangers. Then, in 1979, Thomas A. Munnerlyn's Ranger Press of Austin, Texas, issued a new soft-cover edition of three hundred copies as *Terry's Texas Rangers: Reminiscences of J. K. P. Blackburn.*

Capt. J. K. P. Blackburn died in Tennessee on 6 July 1923, but his memoir of Ranger service remains as one of the most engaging and informative primary accounts of the mounted operations of the Army of Tennessee. As described by Dr. Sam O. Young, a private in John Bell Hood's famed Texas Brigade and later an outstanding Texas journalist and founding editor of the Houston *Post,* Blackburn's reminiscence is "so intensely interesting and charmingly written that I defy anyone to take it up and lay it aside."

Leonidas Banton Giles was born in Montgomery, the

Republic of Texas, on 2 October 1841, the son of Samuel B. and Elizabeth Banton Giles. A student at Baylor University at Independence when the war broke out, he enlisted at Bastrop in Capt. Stephen C. Ferrell's Company D on 7 September 1861.

Giles was wounded in the Rangers' first battle at Woodsonville, Kentucky, on 17 December 1861, the fight in which Col. Benjamin Franklin Terry was killed. Giles recovered to serve through the war, however, and was paroled at Natchez, Mississippi, in May 1865.

Returning to farm in Travis County, he married Anne Watson Battle on 21 March 1866. In addition to farming, Giles spent the post-war years as a captain in the Texas state militia and as Inspector of Immigrants at Laredo.

His memoir was first published in Austin by Von Boeckmann-Jones in 1911 and reprinted in an edition of about five hundred copies by John H. Jenkins's Pemberton Press of Austin in 1967. Although, like Blackburn's reminiscence, it was written some fifty years after the events it portrays, and so is somewhat flawed by failing memory, Texas historian H. Bailey Carroll rightly regarded *Terry's Texas Rangers* as "one of the great recollections of that sterling group of Terry's Texans in the Civil War," as well as "one of the rarest pieces of Texana." The 1911 edition was quoted at $1,000 in a recent price guide to Civil War books.

The year following the publication of *Terry's Texas Rangers*, Giles purchased two hundred acres of land near the LaSalle County community of Cotulla where he farmed until his death ten years later on 12 June 1922.

Ephraim Shelby Dodd, a native of Richmond, Kentucky, moved to Texas in 1857 at age eighteen. After spending some time in Waco with his uncle, James L. McCall, Dodd moved to the Austin home of another uncle, Dr. John R. McCall, and like J. K. P. Blackburn he began to teach school.

In June of 1861, however, soon after Texas left the Union,

Dodd joined Capt. James A. Thompson's company of the Travis Mounted Rifles, a regiment of the Texas Militia, at Walnut Creek in Travis County. In September he transferred to Company D of the Eighth Texas Cavalry. After serving in all of the early campaigns of the Terry Rangers, Dodd was detached from the regiment in order to replace his horse, which had been injured during the summer of 1863. Cut off behind enemy lines when Longstreet abandoned the siege of Knoxville, Dodd was captured in Sevier County, Tennessee, on 17 December 1863.

Imprisoned at Knoxville, after weeks of "freezing and starving by inches," Dodd was tried as a Rebel spy on New Year's Day 1864, the day that his diary was discovered by his Yankee jailers and presented as evidence that he was gathering intelligence about Union positions while passing himself off as a loyal citizen. Although wearing a Mexican serape and a Texas-style hat pinned up with a star cut from a silver peso, an emblem recognized through both armies as the badge of the Texas Ranger, Dodd was also wearing blue trousers and a blue overcoat. This was hardly unusual, "The Yankee quartermaster furnishes us with most of our clothing," Chaplain Bunting remarked.

Sevier County, however, was a hotbed of Unionist sentiment and the scene of particularly brutal internecine warfare. Due to the ferociously partisan nature of the war in east Tennessee, the blue overcoat and a few seemingly innocent lines in his diary were enough to condemn Dodd to death.

Despite pleas for clemency from numerous local citizens, three Union chaplains, and Dodd's fellow Masons, all of whom were convinced of his innocence, Brig. Gen. Samuel P. Carter, Knoxville's provost marshal, ordered Dodd hanged on 8 January 1864. He was one of only fifteen Confederates to be executed by Federal authorities on charges of espionage. "I die innocent of the charge against me," were among his last words.

Not coincidentally, on the day of Dodd's execution, Maj. Gen. John G. Foster, the commander of the Department of the Ohio, issued orders to his unit commanders to "cause to be shot dead all the rebel officers and soldiers (wearing the uniform of the U. S. Army) captured within our lines," and on 17 January forwarded to General Longstreet a transcription of Dodd's court martial, presumably as a warning against further Confederate activity of any sort behind Union lines.

Among Dodd's meager personal effects was his diary, which was appropriated by a lieutenant of a New Hampshire regiment. In January 1914, almost fifty years after its writer was executed, Texas State Librarian Ernest Winkler received a letter from a New York resident who had come into possession of the document when the former Union officer died in 1898. After some negotiation, the diary was purchased for the Texas State Archives. Later that same year it was published by the Austin firm of E. L. Steck as the *Diary of Ephraim Shelby Dodd, Member of Company D, Terry's Texas Rangers, December 4, 1862-January 1, 1864*. It was reprinted in 1979 by the Ranger Press in an edition of two hundred soft-cover copies. This printing, titled the *Diary of E. S. Dodd, Co. D, Terry's Texas Rangers and An Account of His Hanging as a Confederate Spy*, included Chaplain Bunting's commentary on Dodd's "fiendish murder."

Its highly personal entries are hardly the writings of an espionage agent, but they do reveal the character of a courageous, literate, and morally responsible young man who was also keenly observant of his surroundings and circumstances. The Dodd diary, if disappointing to those seeking stirring depictions of battles and leaders, provides a clear window on the daily life and thoughts of a typical Terry Ranger. With the Giles and Blackburn memoirs, it is one of the few first-person accounts of this famed regiment, and together they constitute a basic contribution to any collection of Confederate military history or Texana.

—THOMAS W. CUTRER
Arizona State University West
July 1996

The author of this introduction wishes to extend his thanks to Donaly E. Brice, Supervisor of Reference Services, Department of Archives, Texas State Library, for his expert and cheerful help in researching this and other aspects of Texas military history.

TERRY'S TEXAS RANGERS

BY L.B. GILES

Leonidas Banton Giles, private in Company D 1861-1865.
Wounded at Woodsonville in December 1861. Author of
Terry's Texas Rangers.
Plate 2

INTRODUCTION.

It is but natural that man should desire to leave some record of his achievements for the information of succeeding generations. This desire was manifested in the infancy of the race, and is shown in monuments and chiseled stone, and in writings on skins and reeds.

Here in the South, when the great war of the '60s had terminated and the various actors in the great drama had time to look about them, the desire was universal that the record made by Southern manhood should be perpetuated. The regiment of Texas cavalry known as the "Terry Rangers" shared that feeling; and when the survivors began to meet in annual reunion this desire became manifest. Two propositions appealed to them: one for a history which should tell of their campaigns, their marches, battles, hardships, sufferings; one for a monument which should contain the name of every man who served in the regiment. For reasons which I need not discuss here the plan for the history failed. All funds raised for either purpose were combined into one and placed in control of the monument committee. The equestrian statue which now stands in the grounds of the State Capitol in Austin is the result.

The desire for a narrative still survived, however, discoverable in many personal sketches of events, some taking the form of memoirs, written by various members of the command. I have long contemplated such a work but have felt the lack of ability. It is now perhaps too late to attempt

3

anything like a complete history of the regiment, as the necessary data can hardly be procured. Yet, when my former comrade, D.S. Combs, appealed to me to write something that would supply his children and grandchildren with some knowledge, however imperfect, of the part borne by the Rangers in the great war, I unhesitatingly promised to try it and do the best I could. I wish with all my heart I could make my story as complete as it ought to be, for I firmly believe that a well written narrative of the regiment's wonderful career would be the most entertaining book in the literature of war.

As a first step toward the accomplishment of the task I had undertaken, I wrote to Comrade Combs asking him for such data as he might have or such as his personal recollections might supply; also as to the scope and form of the work as he wished it to appear. His answer is so kind and trusting that I here insert it and, as the lawyers say, make it a part of the record. His letter, written from his home in San Antonio, is dated January 5th:

"My Dear Lee:

"Yours of the 26th of December came duly to hand, and I should have replied sooner but I have been strictly on the go for the last ten days, and I have neglected many things that should have had attention.

"Now, Lee, I wish to state with all the sincerity of my heart, that all I want is plain statements of facts; and while I give you a brief outline of my movements, from the day I was sworn into the service of the Confederate States to the close of the war, I simply do this that you may know where D.S. Combs was, and it is a matter of indifference to me whether my name is mentioned a single time in your story of the doings of the regiment, and, more especially, of the part old Company D played in that drama.

"I was very fearful that the war would be over before I saw a live Yankee. So Charley McGehee and I went fifty miles from home to join a company, and joined Ferrell's company between Bastrop and La Grange. According to my recollection this was in the latter part of August, '61.

"From that day to the day I left the regiment, I was not away from Company D more than ten or twelve days, and then on account of sickness; once at Shelbyville for five or six days; at another time near Nolensville for about the same length of time.

"My initiation was at Woodsonville, and the last of the chapter was at Mossy Creek, Dandridge, and the brick house where N.J. Allen was killed and the artillery duel where Captain Littlefield was wounded. This, I think, was early in January, '64. Here I drew a furlough, and in company with Ike Jones, Bill Fisher and Jeff Burleson, I struck out for home. On my arrival at home my parents and sisters insisted that I ask for assignment to duty on this side of the Mississippi. I had lost one brother by sickness at Searcy, Arkansas, one had been killed at the battle of Chickamauga, one badly wounded at Port Hudson, and another desperately wounded at Mansfield, Louisiana.

"Accordingly, I applied to General E. Kirby Smith for such assignment, and he gave me orders to report to General Magruder at Galveston for assignment to duty in any cavalry command I might select. I chose Colonel J.S. Ford's command on the Rio Grande. I was attached to Captain Carrington's company in Major Cater's battalion, and was with that command in the last fight of the war. This was between Brownsville and the mouth of the Rio Grande, and was about two weeks after General Smith had surrendered the Trans-Mississippi department, but the word had not reached us. I am glad to say that in this last fight of the war the Confederate arms were victorious. A few days after this we got word that the war was over. So we folded our tents and quietly and sadly turned our faces homeward. As a company or battalion we never surrendered. We simply laid down our arms and tried to forget the past and all its disappointments.

"Now to go back and come over the story as it actually occurred, I will simply say that I was never wounded during the war, but particularly unfortunate for my mounts. I had three noble animals killed under me, two at Murfreesboro, one at College Hill, opposite Knoxville, also one wounded at Mt. Washington, near Louisville, Kentucky.

"I was with you at Farmington and at Nolensville, where Ferg Kyle led his line of dismounted men, deployed as skirmishers, up against a solid line of blue, a regiment of infantry, who poured a galling fire into our ranks and caused us to reel and stagger like a drunken man.

"I was with you at Woodsonville, Shiloh, Murfreesboro, Bardstown, Perryville and Chickamauga. Also at Murfreesboro when Forrest with his little band swooped down on the two camps and took them in out of the damp.

"Again, Lee, I will say that I wish you to handle the story in your own way, and I will be perfectly satisfied. What we want is the doings of the *company* and *regiment*. I care not for individual mention. If you and I are satisfied I care not whether others are or not.

"I wish to emphasize this statement. I appreciate more than you know your willingness to undertake this for me, and will gladly remunerate you as far as it is in my power to do for the time you put in on the work.

"Mrs. Combs and I wish to thank you and your daughter for the kind hospitality to us during the reunion, and hope you may both find it convenient to visit us in the near future. Wishing you both a pleasant and prosperous New Year, I am,

"Always yours,

"D.S. Combs."

If I had regretted my promise or had wavered in the slightest from my intention, this letter would have renewed in me the purpose to do my best. Yet I do not see why anyone who writes as well as Comrade Combs should desire another to write for him. I would not, with intention, do injustice to anyone; I know I can not do justice to many deserving the highest praise; but I must say that the regiment had no better soldier than D.S. Combs.

Since this work was well under way Comrade A.B. Briscoe of Company K has kindly placed at my service a large lot of MS. of his personal memoirs. I have used this in several instances, of which due credit is given in the proper places.

Austin, May, 1911.

One of the two known Terry Texas Ranger flags. The flag is in the collection of the Chicago Historical Society. This flag measures 22" x 33", has a field oj dark blue with a white star and the words, "Terry's Texas Ranger's" in gold.
Plate 3

CHAPTER I.

ASSEMBLY AND ORGANIZATION OF THE REGIMENT.

When in 1861 it became evident that war between the sections was inevitable and imminent, B.F. Terry, a sugar planter of Fort Bend county, and Thomas S. Lubbock, of Houston, determined to be in the fight from the start, hurried to Virginia, at their own expense, where they participated in the first battle of Manassas, rendering distinguished services as scouts before the action and in pursuit of the routed enemy afterward. Later the War Department gave them authority to recruit a regiment of Texans for mounted service in Virginia. Returning to Texas they at once issued a call for volunteers.

The conditions were exacting. Each man must furnish his own arms and equipment—a gun of some sort, Colt's repeating pistol, a saddle, bridle and blanket. Notwithstanding these requirements, the response was so prompt that in less than thirty days the ten companies were on their way to the rendezvous at Houston. Some of the companies had the full complement of one hundred men, rank and file, and in a few more days all would have been full. Probably two or more regiments could have been raised at that time if the call had been made.

The personnel was of the very highest. Sons of leading

families, many of them college graduates, professional men, merchants, stockmen, and farmers, served in the ranks as privates, all young, in their teens and early twenties. Rank was scarcely considered. The supreme desire was to get into the war in a crack cavalry regiment.

Since I write without data and from memory only, I must necessarily deal more particularly with the company of which I was a member, known as Company D in the regimental organization. It was recruited largely from Bastrop, with contingents from Hays, Travis and Burleson counties. This organization, full at the beginning, always one of the largest for duty, sustained the greatest loss in killed of all the companies of the regiment. The first officers elected were:

Captain, Stephen C. Ferrell.

First Lieutenant, Charles L. Morgan.

Second Lieutenant, Jesse W. Burdett.

Second Lieutenant, William R. Doak.

The assembly for the company was to be in the town of Bastrop, and notice was given that on a certain morning the march would begin. The men from the adjoining counties reached Bastrop the night before.

It was a bright, sunny August morning. The people, *en masse,* turned out to bid us good-by. Men, women, children, with tears in their eyes, said, "God bless you!" when they clasped our hands as we stood in line. This painful ordeal over, we mounted and rode away on what we believed was a few months' adventure.

Alleyton, sixty miles away, then the terminus of the railroad, was reached without any very exciting adventures. We sent our horses back home and took the train for Houston. The trains were then run to Harrisburg, but we were dumped off in the prairie at Pierce Junction to await a train from Columbia. The hours passed, and the night. We slept little on account of the mosquitoes, which were more numerous and voracious than any I ever met elsewhere. Next morning, as there was still no train, we walked into Houston, a distance of nine miles, pushing by hand the freight car with our saddles and baggage. Here we went into camp in an old warehouse and met some of the other companies.

From McLennan and adjoining counties Captain Thos. Harrison led a company which became Company A. Captain John A. Wharton had a full company raised chiefly in Brazoria and Matagorda counties. It became Company B in the organization and continued the largest in enlistment. Companies C, commanded by Mark Evans; E, by L.N. Rayburn; and I, led by J.G. Jones, were recruited in Gonzales and surrounding counties. Many of these were stockmen and expert horsemen. Company F was from Fayette and commanded by Louis M. Strobel. Company G was from Bexar and Goliad counties. Its first captain was W.Y. Houston. Company H was from Fort Bend county chiefly, and commanded by John T. Holt. Company K, Captain John G. Walker, was from Harris and Montgomery counties, and was full. The word "chiefly" ought to be used in telling where the companies were recruited, for all of them had men from several counties. Here, too, on the 9th of September we were "mustered in," swearing to serve "so long as this war shall last."

From Houston to Beaumont, over a newly constructed railroad, it took nearly all day to make eighty miles. From Beaumont, by steamboat, down the Neches and up the Sabine to Niblett's Bluff; thence a hundred miles on foot, through water much of the way; thence forty miles in carts. It is easy to remember this cart ride. The wheels were six or seven feet high. Motive power, oxen, two pairs to each cart. Engineers, little bow-legged Creoles, each armed with a long, sharp-pointed pole. The vehicles had no springs. As there were no seats, the six or eight passengers in each conveyance had to stand on their feet. At New Iberia, on Bayou Teche, we were transferred to boats, and went down between the beautiful banks of that stream to Brashear, now Morgan City. From there we went through an almost continuous sugar farm to New Orleans. The trip from Houston to New Orleans took over a week. It is now made in less than twelve hours, in a palace car.

In New Orleans we learned that our destination was not Virginia, but Bowling Green, Kentucky, where General A. Sidney Johnston was trying to assemble an army for the defense of that frontier. This was pleasing to us, as General Johnston was a Texan, and personally well known to many of us.

The box cars in which we left New Orleans had been used for shipping cattle, and were not overly clean. Our seats were rough planks without backs. In this luxurious fashion we rode for twenty hours until we reached Nashville. There we encamped in the fair grounds. Ladies in great numbers visited us, and for their entertainment our most expert horsemen gave the first really-truly "wild-west" entertainment ever seen east of the Mississippi.

At Nashville our first death occurred, Thomas Hart, whose loss saddened us greatly. He was a promising young man, not personally known to me.

We had expected to receive our horses here and go on horseback to Bowling Green, but one night Colonel Terry received orders to bring on his regiment "at once." At 1 o'clock in the morning we marched to the station and waited till 2 p.m. for our train. That same afternoon we reached Bowling Green. Our horses were driven through from Nashville by a detail sent back after them. We now received tents, camp utensils and wagons. Here, too, the companies were formally organized into a regiment by the election of the following field officers:

Colonel, B.F. Terry.

Lieutenant Colonel, Thomas S. Lubbock.

Major, Thomas Harrison.

The following staff officers were appointed:

Adjutant, M.H. Royston.

Quartermaster, B.H. Botts.

Commissary, Robert D. Simmons.

Chaplain, R.F. Bunting.

Surgeon, Dr. John M. Weston.

Assistant Surgeon, Dr. Robert E. Hill.

Sergeant Major, W.B. Sayers.

Terry was a native of Kentucky, about 40 years old, of great force of character, firm and self-reliant. His appearance was commanding, and in all ways he was fitted for high rank.

Lubbock was some years older than Terry. He was a native of South Carolina. He was small of stature, pleasant and affable, and made a favorable impression on us. At that time he was in poor health, soon had to go to Nashville for treatment, and we never saw him more.

Harrison was a native of Mississippi. He was a lawyer by profession. A small, nervous, irascible man, who proved to be a fine soldier, became a brigadier general of cavalry, and distinguished himself on many fields.

Winter was now at hand, and the climate was trying on young men raised, as we had been, in the far South. Many fell ill of measles, mumps, pneumonia, and other diseases peculiar to raw levees. Scores went to the hospital, and not a few under the sod. Still the spirits of all, from the youngest private to the resolute colonel, were of the highest, and all were anxious to meet the foe. Such as were able drilled daily, mounted guard, and performed other duties incident to camp life in time of war.

Thomas S. Lubbock accompanied B.F. Terry to Virginia in 1861
and participated in the first battle of Manassas. He and Terry
returned to Texas and organized the Rangers in September 1861.
He was elected Lieutenant Colonel of the Regiment but fell ill in
October and died 9 January 1862, the day after he was
appointed to succeed Terry as Colonel of the regiment. His
brother Francis R. Lubbock was the wartime governor of Texas.
Plate 4

CHAPTER II.

WOODSONVILLE.

Terry, anxious to be doing something, was ordered to lead the regiment to the front on picket and scouting duty. On the 17th of December, Brigadier General Hindman led an expedition to Greene river. When he reached that stream he found the north bank in possession of the enemy's outposts. He deployed some infantry skirmishers, who engaged the enemy at long range but with little effect. Called himself from the immediate front, he left Colonel Terry in charge with instructions to decoy the enemy up the hill and away from support to a point where our infantry and artillery could be used to better advantage.

The enemy allowed themselves to be decoyed, and came across in large numbers. Terry, however, was not the man to invite visitors and then leave someone else to entertain them. Sending Ferrell with about seventy-five men against their left, he led the rest against their right. We charged, yelling, each man riding as fast as his horse could go. Terry fell, dying almost instantly.

Ferrell led his force into an open field against a body of the enemy, who rallied behind a straw stack and such fences as they could find, pouring a galling fire into us. On our part it was a furious but disorderly charge of comparatively undrilled men into one of the best drilled regiments of the Federal army. This was the Thirty-second Indiana Infantry.

15

The officers and men were Germans, who had probably learned their tactics in the old country. They were ignorant of the English language. They were brave fellows, and stood like veterans till shot down.

In view of the great disparity of the forces engaged and the losses sustained, this was one of the most remarkable of all the conflicts of this very remarkable war. One of the very few actions where mounted men engaged infantry on their own ground. It also shows of what stuff the Southern volunteer was made. In support of these statements I invite attention to the official reports. The first is by Colonel Willich. Omitting some unimportant details, it is as follows:

"But now ensued the most earnest and bloody part of the struggle. With lightning speed, under infernal yelling, great numbers of Texas Rangers rushed upon our whole force. They advanced to fifteen or twenty yards of our lines, some of them even between them, and opened fire with rifles and revolvers. Our skirmishers took the thing very coolly, and permitted them to approach very close, when they opened a destructive fire on them. They were repulsed with severe loss, but only after Lieutenant Sachs, who left his covered position with one platoon, was surrounded by about fifty Rangers, several of them demanding of him three times to give up his sword, and let his men lay down their arms. He firmly refused, and defended himself till he fell, with three of his men, before the attack was repulsed.

"Lieutenant Colonel Von Trebra now led on another advance of the center and left flank, when he drew down upon his forces a second attack of the Rangers in large numbers, charging into the very ranks, some dashing through to the rear, which might have proved disastrous.

"In the fight participated three field officers, one staff and sixteen officers of the line, twenty-

three sergeants and 375 men. Our loss is one
officer and ten men dead, twenty-two wounded
and five missing. According to reports of our surgeons several of the wounded are beyond hope of
recovery."

I have omitted from the foregoing interesting and more
or less instructive details of the parts played by Lieutenant
Colonel Von Trebra, Major Snachenberg, Captain Wilchbill-
ing, Adjutant Schmidt, Lieutenant Mank and other heroes
whose names are hard to spell and harder to pronounce.
Valiant men all, and all doubtless recommended for promotion. As will be seen hereafter, to fight with the Rangers was
to be in line of advancement in this world or the next.

I now give General Hindman's report from the Confederate side:

"The firing ceased for about half an hour, and I
went in person to select a suitable place for camp,
leaving Colonel Terry in command, with instructions to decoy the enemy up the hill, where I could
use my infantry and artillery with effect, and be
out of the range of the enemy's batteries.

"Before returning to the column the fire from
the skirmishers recommenced. The enemy appeared in force on my right and center. Colonel
Terry, at the head of seventy-five Rangers, charged
about 300 of the enemy, routed and drove them
back, but fell mortally wounded. A body of the
enemy about the same size attacked the Rangers
under Captain Ferrell on the right of the turnpike,
and were repulsed with heavy loss.*

"My loss in the affair was as follows: Killed,
Colonel Terry and three men of his regiment;

---

* Attack was really made by Ferrell on the enemy,
advancing under command of Von Trebra, as Colonel Willich
reports.—G.

17

dangerously wounded, Lieutenant Morris and three men of the Texas Rangers; slightly wounded, Captain Walker and three men of the Texas Rangers and two men of the First Arkansas battalion."

From General Hindman's report it will be seen that the Rangers had 150 men in the fight, seventy-five with Terry, seventy-five with Ferrell; there being, in fact, two charges. Our loss was twelve altogether. Colonel Willich reported that he had, officers and men, 418 engaged. He had eleven killed, twenty-two wounded and reported five missing, a total of thirty-eight; his missing being prisoners in our hands. Thus 150 men charged 418, inflicting a loss of thirty-eight, sustaining a loss of twelve. Of this number Company D lost five: W.W. Beal and Frank Loftin killed, L.L. Giles mortally wounded, L.B. Giles and John R. Henry slightly wounded.

If a complete record could be obtained I believe a similar disparity of losses would appear in nearly all the engagements in which we bore a part. The splendid horsemanship of our men, and their skill with firearms, made them easily superior to any foe they went against. In this fight our loss was irreparable in the death of our gallant leader. Had he lived he would, without doubt, have reached the highest rank and would have achieved a fame second to none. We had other brave leaders, but none like the matchless Terry.

In the election of officers which followed the death of Terry, Lieutenant Colonel Lubbock was advanced to the command of the regiment, and Captain John G. Walker became lieutenant colonel. Lubbock, who was at that time in bad health, died a few days later. Captain John A. Wharton was chosen to fill his place.

Wharton was a man of ability, of a distinguished family, liberally educated, a lawyer and a captivating public speaker. Enterprising and ambitious, he never forgot during a wakeful moment that the soldier who survived the war would be a voter. He distinguished himself on many fields and became, successively, brigadier general and major general.

About this time Lieutenant Morgan of Company D resigned and Fergus Kyle was elected first lieutenant. Kyle was subsequently promoted to captain, and made a very efficient officer, distinguishing himself on many fields.

The regiment now resumed its duty of guarding the front. The weather was cold, varied with rain, sleet and snow. The men suffered greatly. Some suffering, as to the weather, I escaped, having received a slight wound. I was sent to the hospital at Nashville, Tennessee, where I stayed two days, going from there to the home of a relative, where I spent nearly seven weeks. In the care of my kindred I had all the comforts and some of the luxuries of life. I reported for duty just before the retreat from Bowling Green.

The burial squad informed me that my poor horse, who received some of the lead intended for his master, and yet had no personal interest in the row, had five bullet wounds. He fell under me near the straw stacks. I rode off the field behind John B. Rector, who halted in a shower of bullets and kindly assisted me to mount.

*The battle of Fort Donelson, Tennessee, in February 1862 which
resulted in a loss to the Confederacy. The retreat was covered
by the Terry Texas Rangers.*
Plate 5

CHAPTER III.

RETREAT.

The word is not reassuring to seasoned soldiers. To new troops it is very depressing. Johnston's line was broken on the right at Fishing Creek, and was threatened on the left at Donelson. Bowling Green was, therefore, untenable, and now we must fall back behind the Cumberland.

The Rangers must cover the retreat. It was snowing the morning we left, and the enemy were throwing shells into the place. Our march to Nashville was without incident. We crossed the Cumberland in the night and camped just outside the city. We now learned that Donelson had fallen, and the retreat must be continued. We were ordered down toward Donelson to guard in that direction, and to afford succor to such as had escaped the surrender and might be making their way south.

Returning, we found the army at Murfreesboro, but it moved on by Shelbyville, Huntsville and Decatur to Corinth, Mississippi, the Rangers guarding the rear. The weather was bad and the progress slow, but the enemy did not press us. We crossed the Tennessee river on the railroad bridge, which had been floored for the purpose. When we went into camp rations of bacon and flour were issued to us. Our wagons and camp equipment being somewhere else, we were confronted with the problem of preparing this flour for the immediate consumption of the chronically hungry soldier. If necessity is the mother of invention, hunger is a most capable handmaid of the good dame. An oilcloth is spread on the ground, and on this the flour is kneaded, but how to bake it was the question. Some rolled the dough around a stake or ramrod, which they stuck in the ground by the fire, but the stuff would slip down. Some of us tried a flat rail, and that answered very well. First heating the rail thoroughly, we stuck our biscuits on it, set them before the fire, and watched them brown, our appetites growing keener all the while. The treatment of the bacon was easy. We broiled it on a stick held before the fire or above the coals, and that is the best way it was ever cooked.

At Corinth we had a few days' rest. Absentees came in, and the *morale* improved.

Buell did not follow our line of march, but moved by the more direct route through Franklin, Columbus and Pulaski, intending to unite with Grant at Pittsburg Landing.

CHAPTER IV.

SHILOH.

Johnston planned to attack Grant before the arrival of Buell, and had brought together the largest army ever before assembled in the Confederacy. He had the force under General Hardee from Bowling Green, the remnant of Zollicoffer's army, Bragg from Pensacola with a fine corps of well drilled and well equipped troops, and Polk from Columbus with a light force, altogether nearly 40,000 men. They were to attack an army of veterans flushed with the victory at Donelson.

Johnston ordered the army to move on the morning of April 3, but some of the troops did not get away until that afternoon. It was said that this delay was due to the inexperience of both staff and men. Johnston had intended to attack on the 5th, but the army, delayed by the bad roads, did not arrive in time. Thus we lost twenty-four fateful hours—twenty-four hours of as precious time as was ever lost in war.

Our regiment reached the front on the 4th and was ordered to guard the left wing of the army. In detachments we guarded every road, trail and opening around the whole left front and flank, with strict orders that none of us be allowed to sleep at all. Soon after nightfall it began to rain. It poured down in torrents, and the night was pitch dark. Whether in the saddle, on post or in camp, we could hardly have slept in that downpour. It was a long, dreary night, but morning, a bright spring morning, came at last.

The regiment assembled once more, very wet and uncomfortable. Our arms, too, were wet and, fearing they would fail us in action, we implored Colonel Wharton to let us fire them off. With no thought of possible consequences he consented. Pointing to a wooded hillside, he said:

"Go off there and shoot."

We discharged all the firearms we had. It sounded like a brisk skirmish. The colonel was immediately summoned to headquarters. Camp rumor said that his interview with his superiors was rather stormy, that he was severely reprimanded. It is a fact that on his return he made us a speech, telling us that by yielding to our importunities he had committed a serious blunder which had subjected him to unfavorable criticism by persons in the higher military circles. He seemed to be much perturbed mentally. He asked us to wipe out the stain by our gallant behavior in the coming engagement; asked us to ride further into the enemy's ranks than any other regiment. I think most of us audibly promised to do what he asked; and we kept the promise as far as circumstances would permit, as will be seen.

The whole army had arrived by Saturday afternoon. Early Sunday morning, April 6th, the forward movement began. The enemy were either in bed or preparing breakfast, and were taken by surprise. I know the surprise has been denied by so eminent a person as General Grant, but as he was sleeping at Savannah, nine miles away, he is hardly a competent witness. Thousands of us saw camp kettles and coffeepots on the fires, beds just as the occupants had left them, blankets spread and clothing strewn about.

It is not my purpose to describe the battle of Shiloh. I wish merely to speak of some principal incidents. It was a continuous advance of the Confederates nearly all of the day, Sunday. The roar of big guns and the rattle of musketry was unceasing.

The Rangers were kept in column just in the rear of the left wing, and had no part in the conflict till late in the day, when our eagerness to take part in the fight was gratified by an order to clear our extreme left, and assail the enemy, who was then retiring through thick woods.

We had to cross a muddy branch. At first two abreast could get over, but it soon became so bad that only one at a time could cross, and then it was a good long jump for a horse. Not half of the regiment was over when the leading files rushed up the hill through a small open field. Turning to the right they came to a high rail fence behind which was a line of blue. From this line came a most destructive fire which emptied many saddles. John Crane of Company D was killed. Clint Terry, a new arrival, brother of our former colonel, fell mortally wounded.

We were too few to make any impression, although some of our men dismounted and began throwing down the fence. A few even crossed into the wood. The firing was so hot that we beat a hasty retreat in spite of the appeals of Colonel Wharton and other officers, who did all they could to stop our flight. We didn't stop until we were out of range, when we re-formed at once. Thus our second encounter with the enemy met with a repulse. I may say, however, that this charge, if it be proper to call it a charge, was not without good results to our cause. Several years since I received a letter from Colonel Chisholm, who was then on the staff of General Beauregard. He wrote that it was he who led the regiment in that advance; that the object of it was to detain the enemy until other troops could be brought up; that for this purpose the movement was measurably successful.

That afternoon we learned with sorrow of the death of General Johnston. This we then regarded as a great calamity, and time has not changed our opinion.

We were not engaged again that day. We spent the night

on the battlefield, amid the dead of the enemy, subsisting ourselves and our horses from the abundant supplies on every hand. Though it rained another downpour, and though we had no shelter, we slept as only tired soldiers can.

Reinforced by Buell's 40,000, the enemy assumed the offensive next day. The Confederates only resisted, as best they could, to get off their wounded, their trains and artillery, over muddy roads. The Rangers were dismounted to aid in resisting the forward movement, losing several men. John H. Washington of Company D was shot through the hips and left on the field for dead; but under the care of Federal surgeons he recovered, and is living today.

Tuesday, the 8th, two companies of the Rangers, under Major Harrison, with part of Forrest's men, all under the command of Forrest, made a brilliant charge on a mounted force of the enemy, believed to be a large escort of a general officer, and ran them back to the main force of infantry.

The pursuit now ceased and, without further molestation, we returned to Corinth. Here we remained two or three weeks, and received some recruits, the first since leaving Texas. Company D got six, T.A.W. Hill, William and A.J. Kyle, George T. McGehee, T.M. Rector and S.M. Watkins. They were quite an addition to our force. All were fine soldiers and continued to the end. There was much sickness, caused by bad water. Everybody was anxious for more active service.

The regiment was now ordered into Tennessee. Crossing the river at Lamb's Ferry, we captured a detachment of the enemy, guarding a railroad bridge, after a hot fight, in which we lost several men. Captain Harris of Company I was killed; also William DeWoody of Company D. There is one incident of this affair which I shall never forget. Among our prisoners was a captain of an Ohio regiment. He had six bullet wounds in his body. He sat up in the boat as we crossed the river, and walked unassisted up the hill on the other side.

CHAPTER V.

FORREST AT MURFREESBORO.

We were now ordered to Chattanooga. Here we were placed in a brigade under the command of Colonel N.B. Forrest. At this time but little was known of this great soldier. He had not then become famous, and there were not wanting officers of high rank who predicted disaster as the result of his operations. Without the advantages of education, he possessed strong common sense, unfaltering courage, energy that never flagged, and unbounded confidence in himself. Under his leadership our metal was not to grow rusty for lack of employment.

Setting out from Chattanooga on the 8th of July, we crossed the Tennessee river and the Cumberland mountains into middle Tennessee. On the 11th we reached McMinnville and remained until the afternoon of the 12th. Here Forrest made his regimental commanders acquainted with his plans. His objective was Murfreesboro, over forty miles away, garrisoned by a force of the enemy estimated at 2000 men, under the command of Brigadier General Crittenden.

Late in the afternoon we started for an all night ride. At Woodbury we halted and fed our horses, resuming the march at midnight. We reached the vicinity of Murfreesboro at daylight on the 13th.

Now occurred one of those unfortunate blunders which often mar the best laid plans; probably made by Forrest himself. Colonel Wharton with the Rangers was to attack a camp of the enemy on the Liberty pike north of town. Forrest, who had been riding at the head of the column, turned aside to allow us to pass. When six companies had gone by he fell in with his staff and escort. Thus it happened that nearly half of the regiment followed Forrest into the town and out to the westward. The courthouse was garrisoned by a company of the Ninth Michigan Infantry, who poured a hot fire into our ranks from the windows. Forrest and the Rangers rode on, but the sound of firing had aroused the good ladies from their beds; looking out they saw the dear defenders of their cause. Without taking time for very elaborate toilets, they rushed into the streets just as the Georgians came up. Pointing to the courthouse, they begged them to attack the hated foe. With a "Hurrah for the women!" these perfectly green troops dismounted, broke down the doors, and captured the garrison, but with severe loss.

When Forrest discovered that he had with him only a handful of Rangers, he turned back to look after the rest of his command. Captain Ferrell, now the ranking officer, led us through the suburbs of the town towards the right, or north where he thought to find the regiment. While we were passing through a field of standing corn, the artillery of the enemy opened on us at short range. The first shot struck William Skull of Company G, taking off both legs and passing through his horse, killing both instantly.

We found the main part of the regiment about half a mile east of the town, on the road by which we had come. They had made a spirited attack on the enemy, but were too weak to get any favorable results, and had retired, Wharton being wounded. As soon as the regiment was united Wharton sent the adjutant, M.H. Royston, and ten men to report to Forrest for orders. I was of this party. We found Forrest in town. He spoke with some show of irritation:

"Tell him to bring his men up here."

During all this time he had been attacking the enemy with the forces at hand, but there was little result of a decisive nature.

Some of his chief officers had advised him to be content with what he had already accomplished and withdraw; but he was not of the withdrawing kind. Preparing for a final assault, when the Rangers came up, he delayed the attack long enough to send a demand for surrender to the camp of the Michigan regiment. This was promptly agreed to. He now sent a like demand to the Third Minnesota. Colonel Lester of that regiment asked for an hour's time and an opportunity to consult with Colonel Duffield. This officer was seriously wounded. Forrest allowed half an hour and the privilege of the interview. As Lester was going to the room of Colonel Duffield opportunity was given him to see our strength. When the half hour was up he surrendered his entire force.

The troops surrendered consisted of fifteen companies of infantry, six of the Ninth Michigan and nine of the Third Minnesota; seven companies of cavalry, four of the Fourth Kentucky and three of the Seventh Pennsylvania; and two sections (four guns) of Hewett's battery: in all 1765 men.

The brigade commander, General Crittenden, was found hiding in a room at a tavern.

The spoil was immense; a large number of wagons, with military stores and equipment of all sorts.

The merits of this enterprise are very great, but it must be admitted that had the enemy all been together, under a resolute commander, they could have beaten us. They had nearly 1800 men of all arms, infantry, cavalry and artillery— a miniature army—while Forrest had a little over 1300 men, some of them absolutely green troops.

In regard to this affair, General Buell, commanding the department, published a very caustic order, of which a short extract is here given:

"Take it in all its features, few more disgraceful

examples of neglect of duty and lack of good conduct can be found in the history of wars. It fully merits the extreme penalty which the law provides for such conduct. The force was more than sufficient to repel the attack effectually."

CHAPTER VI.

MANY MARCHES AND SKIRMISHES—THE KENTUCKY CAMPAIGN.

We rested at McMinnville three or four days, and then started a hard ride with little rest for Lebanon, a distance of fifty miles, intending to surprise and capture a force of 500 cavalry stationed there. On the morning of the 20th we dashed into the place, but the enemy had been warned and had left in a hurry for Nashville.

We remained one day and night in this beautiful little city, recipients of the unbounded hospitality of its splendid people. They fed us on poultry, roast pig, ham, cakes and pies like "mother used to make," and filled our haversacks for the march.

From Lebanon our route was by "The Hermitage," so long the home of Andrew Jackson. Here a short halt was made, and many of the men visited the house and grounds. Mounting, we moved on to Stone river, seven miles from Nashville, where a small picket force was captured. Thence we crossed over to the Murfreesboro turnpike, only four miles from the city, and destroyed four railroad bridges, capturing the guards—in all about 120 men. We then turned off in the direction of Lebanon, and camped for the night after riding for a few miles; here we paroled our prisoners. Passing around Murfreesboro we marched to McMinnville, where we rested till the 10th of August.

We then advanced to the line of railroad, captured the pickets and burned a few bridges. The enemy had now begun to erect stockades for their guards at the bridges. There was one not yet finished, and Forrest tried to capture it but failed. Captain Houston of Company G was killed in this attack.

Moving in the direction of Altamont we camped in a cove near the mountain. The enemy advanced in force on all the roads. We had to take the dry bed of a creek which ran parallel to one of the roads on which the enemy was advancing. We traveled in this creek a mile or two, and then emerged into the open. A battery of the enemy, on the McMinnville road, not more than 600 yards away, opened fire upon us. The very best of troops, who will charge anything, are often thrown into a panic by an attack from an unexpected quarter. We broke into a run and were soon out of range, though in considerable disorder.

Marching leisurely to Sparta, we joined forces with Bragg's army, then on the move into Kentucky. Forrest was ordered to guard the left flank and harass the rear of the enemy in his retreat to Nashville. We came up to their rear guard at Woodbury, and chased them clear up to Murfreesboro, but could only run them through the place.

Bragg soon moved by Glasgow and on to Mumfordsville, getting in ahead of Buell and on his line of march. He had a strong position, but for some unaccountable reason turned off and let the Federal army pass on to Louisville. Forrest kept on the left and in close touch with the enemy till the army turned aside, when we went on to the vicinity of Louisville. Forrest was now relieved and ordered to Tennessee, and Colonel John A. Wharton was placed in command of the brigade. We kept close up to Louisville, in observation of the enemy's movements. Had a small but spirited skirmish at Mt. Washington, as related in the introduction.

Early in October Buell began to move with some vigor. An enterprising brigade of cavalry got between us and our main army. They took position at Bardstown and thus we were "cut off." When intelligence of this move reached Wharton he called in his outposts, threw his command into column, Rangers in front, Company D leading. At a gallop we started for the seat of trouble. The enemy had chosen a strong position at the mouth of the lane in which we were traveling, and had their courage been equal to their enterprise they could have given us a warm entertainment. When we came in sight of them our bugle sounded the charge and we went at them as fast as our horses could carry us. They broke almost at once, firing only a few shots. It was now a chase for miles. We caught over 200 of them, and strewed the woods with their dead and wounded. General George H. Thomas, of the Federal army, says they lost about "twenty killed and wounded, and a great many missing"; these "missing" were our prisoners. Our loss was small—I can not recall the casualties. It was one of the softest snaps in the way of a fight that we had during the war.

Some amusing incidents nearly always occur, but the laughter rarely takes place till all danger is past. After the long chase we, as well as the enemy, were very much scattered. John B. Rector seeing a lone Federal, rushed up and demanded his surrender. "Surrender yourself," replied the man, leveling his pistol. Now Rector had discharged every chamber of his pistol and promptly complied. Just then Bill Davis dashed up. He was a large, fierce looking man, on a powerful horse not less than sixteen and a half hands high. He broke out, "John, why the—-don't you disarm that—— —— Yankee?" "I am a prisoner myself, Bill." Quick as a flash Davis was at the fellow's side and bringing his pistol against his head broke out, "Give up them pistols, you —- —— blue-bellied —- —-." The shooting irons were promptly handed over and the prisoner escorted to the rear.

33

In the language of the great American game it was pure "bluff" all around for all the firearms were empty, but Bill Davis was always loaded to the muzzle with quick firing profanity which he could discharge in rattling volleys on the slightest provocation. I am glad to say, however, that he no longer goes loaded thus, for he has been a strict churchman for several years.

General Bragg published a general order highly laudatory of the Rangers for this affair, but I have found no record of it. It was read to the regiment and complimented us in high terms.

Bragg's army was widely dispersed, gathering supplies in that fertile section. Buell was pressing him, and to get time for concentration, and to get his train out of the way, we made a stand at Perryville, where, on the 8th of October, was fought one of the fiercest combats of the war. Fourteen thousand Confederates kept at bay for nearly two days the immense army of the enemy, but with heavy loss to both sides. Wharton's brigade held the extreme right and did a full share of the fighting. Among our killed was Major Mark Evans of the Rangers. Captain Ferrell of Company D succeeded him, and Lieutenant Kyle of Company D became captain.

I was in the battle of Perryville, not with the regiment, but in a small detachment on the left while the Rangers were on the right. Hence I avail myself of the description of "Perryville" given by A.B. Briscoe, who kindly placed his "Personal Memoirs" at my service.

> "The enemy was on the west side of the creek and our army on the east. The valley between was open field and the tops of the hills covered in places with timber. It was an ideal battlefield; there were no breastworks, but the hills on both sides were crowned with artillery. Polk was in command of the Confederate forces and expected the enemy to

attack and waited for them until about 2 p.m. In the meantime the artillery was making the very earth tremble with a duel of nearly 100 guns. We lay in a little valley a few hundred yards to the rear, partially sheltered from this storm of shells. At 2 p.m. we were moved in column through the lines of infantry and the smoking batteries to the front. The open valley was before us with a deep creek spanned by a wooden bridge. Down we charged in column of fours across the bridge. After crossing, each squadron formed left front into line, which made us present five lines, one behind the other, and in this order we charged up the hill, into the woods and among the Yankees. This whole movement was made in a sweeping gallop and as if on parade. How different from the way we were handled at Shiloh! The Yankees were brushed back from the hill and woods and when the bugle sounded the recall and we returned, our own infantry and artillery had crossed the creek and were taking position on the hills from which we had driven the enemy. But again we had lost our commander, the gallant Lieutenant Colonel Mark Evans, who fell mortally wounded at the head of the regiment."

I have copied this literally, but I am of the opinion that Evans was only major.

Bragg had secured the needed time. He now started for Cumberland Gap, leaving the cavalry to protect his rear and retard, as best they could, the onward march of the enemy. Colonel Joseph Wheeler was made chief of cavalry and had command of all in the rear. The country was timbered, broken, not very fertile, affording little in the way of food for man or beast. We had to form line and skirmish several times a day. The service was very trying. For more than a week there was no order to unsaddle.

At last Buell gave up the pursuit and started to Nashville.

We went on through Cumberland Gap to Knoxville, where we had a snowstorm. From Knoxville, by Kingston and over the mountains, we went to Sparta, Murfreesboro and Nolensville. At Nolensville we had a position on the left of the army. Here some promotions were announced. Colonel Wharton became a brigadier general, his commission dating from the Bardstown fight, the 4th of October. Harrison became colonel, Ferrell, lieutenant colonel, and Gustave Cook, major. Ferrell was soon compelled to resign on account of bad health. Cook then became lieutenant colonel and S. Pat Christian, major. In Company D, Dechard became first lieutenant and W.R. Black, second lieutenant.

We remained at Nolensville nearly two months, picketing and scouting. We passed our second Christmas, a serious and sober set, thinking of the homes and loved ones far away, and wondering if we should ever see them again.

CHAPTER VII.

MURFREESBORO.

The enemy did not allow us much time for repining. Promptly on the 26th they moved out in force. We were sent forward to develop their strength. The regiment, under the command of Captain Kyle, was drawn up in a field and dismounted. Our leader conducted us over a high rail fence into an open wood of cedar trees. We went along listening to his encouraging words until we reached the top of a slight rise. Just over the crest was a solid line of infantry lying down. Kyle at once ordered a retreat. At least that's what he meant, though the words he actually used are not in the manual. He said:

"Get out of here, men! There's a whole brigade!"

We understood him and so did the Yankees, who sprang to their feet and delivered a volley, doing little damage. The high fence had not seemed a serious obstacle as we went in, but when I got back to it on the return, with bullets striking it like hail on a roof, it looked very formidable. I sprang up on it and just fell off on the other side. When I got up the command was moving off rapidly. I had started to the rear as soon as the others, but they outran me, and I didn't "throw" the race either. I turned to the left, down the line of fence, climbed another, and was now reasonably safe but nearly exhausted. I had still to go half a mile before I reached the command. My saddle felt mighty good and restful.

It was now plain that it was a general advance of the

enemy, and Bragg prepared for the battle of Murfreesboro, whither we now marched promptly. In the line Wharton's brigade occupied the left. When the ball opened in earnest he led this command around the right of the enemy's line, and within 600 yards of Rosecrans' headquarters attacked and captured a wagon train going to the rear. We could not hold it long; but we captured a four-gun battery and held on to that; moved down toward Nashville and ran into the train again.

In these operations Company D lost two killed, Sam Friedberger and Wayne Hamilton. Kenner Rector was wounded. John W. Hill and P.J. Watkins were made prisoners. Hill's horse was killed as we were retiring before superior numbers. He was away three or four months, and greatly missed, for he was a good one.

After a strenuous day of it, with a good many prisoners and the four guns, we returned to the army and were sent to the right, taking position on the right of Breckenridge's line. We saw that gallant officer and his splendid division move forward through an open field with the precision of parade, under a furious cannonading from the Federal batteries strongly posted in a cedar wood. The shells plowed great gaps through their ranks. When the colors fell other hands seized them and bore them onward. When they reached the position of the enemy they wavered and began to give way, in order at first, but as they retreated under a distressing fire of artillery and musketry, they broke into a run. We stood there and could not help them, although every man of us would have gone to their aid with a whoop.

This charge deserves to rank with Malvern Hill, Franklin, and other useless sacrifices of life. Like the charge of the light brigade, "it was magnificent, but it was not war."

This was Bragg's final effort, and he withdrew from the contest. The only tactics he seems to have learned was to wait till the enemy came up to his lines and fortified himself;

then attack and lose more men than the enemy, then sneak away. He had heard somewhere that "he who fights and runs away may live to fight another day."

Bragg stopped at Shelbyville. Rosecrans was content to stay at Murfreesboro, begging his government for more cavalry; nor did he feel safe in advancing till he had a large addition to his mounted force.

We took position on the left of the army, picketing and scouting the front, with occasional skirmishes and reconnoissances [*sic*].

John A. Wharton was the first Captain of Company B. He became colonel of the regiment in January 1862. He was later promoted to General and by 1864 was serving under General Taylor in the Trans-Mississippi theater. He was killed by Colonel G.W. Baylor in a personal quarrel on 6 April 1865.
Plate 6

CHAPTER VIII.

THE DONELSON TRIP AND RETREAT
TO CHATTANOOGA.

Just who conceived this wild-goose chase, I am not informed. For suffering, hardships, and barrenness of results, it is only exceeded by Napoleon's Russian campaign. On the 25th of January, General Wheeler, in command of the brigades of Wharton and Forrest, took up the line of march for Dover, or Fort Donelson. I do not know how to describe the weather, except in the language of the grammar on the comparison of adjectives: cold, colder, coldest. We crossed one little stream fifteen or twenty times in one day. The water froze on the legs of our horses until they were encased in ice above the knees; their tails were solid chunks of ice, while we had to walk to keep warm. Men and horses suffered intensely.

When we reached the vicinity of Dover, Forrest reported to Wheeler that he had but a scant supply of ammunition; and investigation disclosed the fact that Wharton's brigade was little better off in this regard. Forrest did not hesitate to advise withdrawal of our forces without attempt at action, but Wheeler determined to proceed.

Forrest attacked from the north and east, carried the enemy's outer works, and drove them into the redoubts, but with great loss of life. His ammunition was now exhausted, and he was compelled to fall back. Wharton attacked from the Donelson side, and captured one brass field gun, but he, too, was compelled to retire because his ammunition was running low. The Rangers had been sent out on the Fort Henry road before these operations were begun and so had no part in the assault.

Jordan, in his "Life of Forrest," says:

"The Confederate losses were heavy. Forrest had one-fourth of his force, or 200 of his officers and men killed, wounded and captured, and Wharton's casualties did not fall short of sixty killed and wounded."

Now the retreat began. All the command, except the Rangers, practically out of ammunition. The weather did not moderate. The second or third night a report reached Wheeler that a heavy column of the enemy, cavalry and infantry, under General Jeff C. Davis, had left Nashville to head him off. About midnight we were ordered to saddle up. It was so cold that if we touched a gun-barrel or bridle bit our hands stuck to the metal, and we had to put those bits into the mouths of our poor horses.

We reached Duck river about daylight, and found it bank full, the surface covered with floating ice. After some search a ford was found and we crossed to the south side. As Davis' command did not show up, we went into camp and warmed ourselves a little. After a rest of a day or two we moved leisurely back to our old position.

I do not know what could have been accomplished by this expedition beyond the capture of a small garrison. Certainly the suffering and the losses of men and horses were very great. For a long time when the men wanted to reach the superlative of suffering they spoke of the Donelson trip.

In April we moved over to the right and camped a few days at Sparta. The regiment captured a mail train between Murfreesboro and Nashville, getting about a dozen officers.

The men rifled the mail sacks and amused themselves reading the letters of the Yankees. They obtained also a considerable amount of greenbacks; also a silver-mounted pistol, said to belong to General Rosecrans. My horse was lame and so I missed this expedition—and my share of the greenbacks.

Toward the last of June the Federal army, having received reinforcements, including heavy additions to its cavalry force, began another forward movement. The Rangers were dismounted to skirmish with the advance. During this action a heavy rainstorm came up; we thought this would suspend the affair, but when the rain ceased we found the Yankees had advanced their lines considerably. Regarding this as a violation of the rules of the game, we mounted and rode off.

Their cavalry now showed unusual spirit and audacity, pressing us pretty close. On the 4th of July, at the site of the present University of the South, the Rangers had to charge and drive them back. The retreat was continued across the mountains and the Tennessee river to Chattanooga.

The Rangers took position at Rome, Georgia. There we had a few weeks' needed rest and recruited our jaded horses. Roasting ears were in season, fruit was beginning to ripen, and so we feasted on good things. The runabouts—"pie rooters" we called them—made the best of their opportunities. Bill Arp said they found every road in the county, and then some.

Dr. Bunting, our chaplain, started a series of meetings, and many embraced the opportunity to pledge themselves to the better life. The boys, from their scant pay, contributed money to buy a horse for General John A. Wharton. The presentation speech was made by John B. Rector, Wharton replying. Both speakers pledged the last drop of their blood, etc. Same old story, but a trifle stale by this time.

CHAPTER IX.

CHICKAMAUGA.

Rosecrans maneuvered Bragg out of Chattanooga. He now seemed to have a contempt for his adversary, and divided his army into three columns in an effort to bring ours to bay. One crossed the mountains and took position at Alpine, forty miles south of the center, evidently to gain the rear of the Confederates.

We were sent to look after this column. Lieutenant Baylor of the Rangers reported to Wharton that a heavy force of infantry was at Alpine. Wharton reported this to Bragg with a note vouching for Baylor's reliability. Bragg broke out:

"Lieutenant Baylor lies; there is no infantry south of us!"

In a day or two, however, he became convinced that the report was true, and made some feeble effort to attack them in detail. Nothing came of it except that Rosecrans, who now discovered that his enemy was not retreating so precipitately, took the alarm and began to concentrate his widely separated columns. The force at Alpine had to cross the mountains. It took them two days to get to the center, now menaced by the Confederates. Imagine Stonewall Jackson in Bragg's place!

Of the larger events of the battle of Chickamauga I shall treat very briefly. It has been truthfully called the soldiers' battle. Whatsoever of strategy or generalship there had been had miscarried and two armies stood face to face for a trial of strength; a test of manhood. The numbers were about equal, not far from 70,000 on a side. The Federals had the advantage of position, which they had fortified. The Confederates had to attack. Never was fiercer attack and defense. Never was shown greater courage.

The enemy were driven from their works, but with frightful loss to the Confederates. Their killed numbered 2389. The wounded 13,412; while the Federals' loss in killed was 1656, wounded, 9769. It was such dearly bought and fruitless victories as this which finally defeated the South.

The Terry Rangers were on the extreme left of the line and were ordered to drive the enemy from their front. This order was executed in handsome style. The enemy proved to be our old antagonists, the Third Ohio Cavalry. After the charge a message was brought to Lieutenant Dechard, of the Rangers, that a wounded Federal officer wished to see him. He rode to the spot and dismounted. When he saw the wounded man, he said:

"Why, it's my old friend, Major Cupp. I am sorry to see you thus."

"Lieutenant Colonel Cupp," replied the other, "but I've had my last promotion. You people have got me this time."

More than a year before, these officers, each a lieutenant in command of an escort for a flag of truce, had met. They met again, a few weeks later, under the same circumstances, but Cupp was now a captain. After the fight in Bardstown Dechard was in command of the guard for the prisoners, and recognized his former acquaintance.

"Captain Cupp, I am glad to see you," said he.

"Major Cupp," corrected the prisoner, "but I can not say that I glad to see you under the circumstances."

As the cartel was still in force, he was soon exchanged, and as we have seen when he fell, Dechard was near. These facts were related to me by Dechard himself, and he was known to be perfectly reliable. These incidents confirm the old adage, "Truth is stranger than fiction."

The dying officer desired Dechard to take his watch and other belongings and send them to his relatives in Ohio, which was done a few days later by flag of truce.

Wheeler and Forrest followed the discomfited Federals up to Chattanooga. Here it was remembered that two detachments under Lieutenants Friend and Batchelor had been left on picket in gaps of the mountain away to the left of the battlefield, and I was ordered to go to them at once and direct them to join the command, which would be found on the Athens road.

There was about an hour of daylight, and I hoped to pass the ground of the terrible struggle before night, knowing that there was nothing for me or my horse until I did so. In this I was disappointed. Darkness came on shortly after I reached the scene of that awful carnage. Many of the Federal dead and wounded still lay where they had fallen. The air was freighted with a horrible odor, the battlefield's commentary on war. The wounded hearing my horse's footfalls, began calling me to give some assistance. Dismounting I picked my way to the first one. He desired to be turned over. Another wanted his canteen. The poor fellow had struggled while there was strength, and now unable to move further, was out of reach of his canteen. These were relieved and others not specially remembered here. It seemed that hundreds were calling. I was ever a coward in the presence of suffering, besides duty required that I should proceed on my journey. So I asked:

"Are you aware that your own surgeons with their details and ambulances are here uncontrolled on the field?"

"Oh, yes," was the answer, "they come around every day and leave us water, a little food and medicine, but it is awful to lie here this way."

I mounted and rode off, feeling sad at the fate of these men dying unattended hundreds of miles from home and loved ones, but I steeled my heart by the thought that if they had stayed at home with their loved ones they would not be thus dying.

I was now lost. It was dark and my horse could not follow any road, for roads were everywhere. Artillery wheels make many roads on a battlefield. After a while I saw a light and went to it. It was the camp fire of the details for the care of the wounded. These men sat around. The ambulances and mules were near. There was a little house, too. On the porch I saw some officers in uniform. Surgeons they were. I inquired for some resident. A slender girl came to the door and in reply to my request directed me to Lee and Gordon's mill.

The moon was now rising. I was on that part of the field from which the dead and wounded had been removed, but there was wreck and ruin everywhere. Maimed and groaning horses, and no one to waste a load of ammunition to end their suffering; broken gun carriages, the debris of a battlefield.

I crossed and watered my horse in the stream at the mill. As I rode up the hill I met two of my own company, who had been at the wagon camp cooking for the company. When they learned how far it was to the command and the horrors of the battlefield, they readily agreed to camp, for it was now late. So I had supper, for my comrades had sacks of bread and bacon, but my poor horse had nothing. We lay down and slept under the shining moon, although but a few miles away hundreds of human beings lay dying.

On the morrow I proceeded on my journey. When I reached the first detachment under Lieutenant Friend and delivered my message, he kindly sent one of his men on to tell Batchelor: gave me some forage for my horse, and all gathered around anxious for news of the battle. Here they had been in sound of the mighty struggle, the boom of the great guns, even the rattle of small arms, while their comrades were in dire peril, but denied the privilege of sharing in their danger or triumph. They had heard that the enemy had been driven from the field, but had heard nothing from their own command. They were hungry for news from the Rangers. What part they took, and who were killed or wounded? For they knew if the Rangers had been engaged somebody was hurt.

These occurrences took place nearly forty-eight years ago, and yet their memory is clear in my mind, and when I think of my lonely ride in Chickamauga's gloomy woods, of the dead and dying, the wreck and ruin of that awful night, I am convinced that there is no more expressive definition of war than General Sherman has given.

When Batchelor's squad came up we started to overtake the command, joining it on the following day, as well as I remember. It was then well on its way to the Federal rear in middle Tennessee.

CHAPTER X.

WHEELER'S GREAT RAID.

Our march was up the Holston river to find an unguarded ford, but the pickets were everywhere. We halted in a field at night, and Company D, armed with picks and spades, was directed to go to the river bank and there make a way for the artillery. A guide from the vicinity showed us a way across, by a ford unknown to the Yankees. We captured a few pickets.

Wheeler now divided his forces, himself leading a column into Sequatchie valley, where he captured and burned 2000 wagons. He then overtook the remainder of the command as we descended the mountains. Our route was by McMinnville and Murfreesboro, and the way was sufficiently familiar to us, since we had traveled it so often under Forrest the year before.

When we reached the vicinity of Murfreesboro, Captain Kyle with his squadron, consisting of Companies D and F, was ordered to ride around the place, reach the railroad leading to Nashville, and try to capture a train. We came to the railroad a little before daylight, but there were no trains running: the enemy had learned that the "rebels" were in the country. Captain Kyle heard of a lot of wagons down toward Nashville and decided to take them in. This he did without resistance. The teams had been engaged in hauling wood to the garrison at Nashville, and the wagons were drawn by oxen, the only instance of this kind that we saw during the war. The oxen being fat, and also too slow of foot to go with us in any other form, were converted into beef.

We crossed over to Shelbyville pike, the scene of some of our operations in the spring. Learning that a small force of cavalry held Shelbyville, General Wharton ordered the Rangers to attempt their capture. We saddled up early, and rode briskly, reaching there about daylight, but the enemy had left. There were several stores in this place, established by some enterprising Yankees, and stocked with clothing and dry goods. Rather than have their doors broken down, the owners opened them. Winter was coming on, we were a long way from home and nearly naked, and here was our chance for winter supplies. Some of the boys got a black "Prince Albert" coat. This was presented to the chaplain, who wore it a long time.

The line of march led by Farmington. Here the enemy had taken a strong position in a cedar thicket. Over the ground were scattered large boulders. The enemy, armed with Spencer rifles, were lying behind these stones. The Rangers were ordered to charge this position. We got up pretty close; in fact, into the edge of the thicket; but they poured such a destructive fire into us that it did not take us long to discover that we had more than we could handle. We took some prisoners. We also got some of these rifles, the first of the kind I had ever seen; they would shoot seven times without reloading. The casualties are not remembered, except that Major Christian and Lieutenant Blackburn were wounded. Love, of Company C, was killed.

That night at headquarters they were discussing the incidents of the day. Wharton said the Rangers had done all that any soldiers could do; that it was impossible for mounted troops to drive brave men, armed as were the enemy, from such a position. General Wheeler said they had done all that he expected; had held the enemy engaged while our artillery and wagons ran by through a field, thus saving the command from a bad situation. Then Colonel Harrison spoke:

"It was no fight at all! I'm ashamed of them! If they can not do better than that I'll disown them!"

A staff officer put in:

"I always thought that regiment somewhat overrated anyhow."

This aroused "old Tom," who got up, shook his finger in the fellow's face and broke out furiously:

"Who the —- are you? There is not a man in that regiment who can not kick you all over this yard, sir!"

As he strode off to his horse, he was heard to say:

"By —- I'll curse them all I want to; but I'll be —- if anybody else shall do it in my presence!"

Moving on to the Tennessee river, we crossed that stream at one of the fords along the Mussel Shoals. From there, in a more leisurely manner, we went back to the army, still besieging the Federals at Chattanooga.

Thomas Harrison was Captain of Company A briefly before being appointed Major of the regiment in October 1861. He succeeded Wharton as Colonel of the regiment in November 1862 and served almost two years in that position before becoming a brigade commander and receiving a promotion to Brigadier General in January 1865. During the war he was wounded three times, once severely, and had five horses killed from under him.

Plate 7

CHAPTER XI.

EAST TENNESSEE CAMPAIGN.

Bragg felt so sure that Rosecrans would be starved into surrender that he dispatched Longstreet to Knoxville to take in the garrison stationed there. Our division, commanded by General Martin, was sent along with him. Longstreet laid siege to the place. We were transferred from one side of the river to the other, fording the freezing water at night. We had a little skirmish on College hill; details not remembered, except that Lieutenant Black was wounded.

It was reported that the "loyal" people up the river were in the habit of loading small boats with provisions, setting them adrift to float down the river for the use of the garrison in Knoxville, the boats being caught by a boom across the stream. Someone conceived the brilliant idea that if trees were cut down and rolled into the river above, they would float down and break the boom. Our regiment, placed temporarily under the command of somebody's staff officer anxious to distinguish himself, was detailed for this service. A worse selection could hardly have been made for the performance of such work. Probably not one man in twenty was possessed with any skill with the ax. Young men raised on the prairies, professional men, boys from the stores, sons of planters, who had slaves to do their chopping, composed this force of axmen. Night, a very dark night at that, was the time selected for the exploit. A light drizzle was falling.

55

Imagine anybody trying to cut down trees under such circumstances! The staff colonel in command stopped at a
house where there was a blazing fire, dismounted, and took
a comfortable seat. The regiment went up on the hillside and
hacked away for hours. I believe some trees were actually
felled, chopped into convenient lengths, and rolled into the
stream and appeared to sink in the water. All suffered from
the cold. It was such foolish services as this that tended to
demoralize the Confederate soldier and sap a man's courage
and patriotism as nothing else will. There is something
inspiring in a charge, albeit there is danger, too, with comrades falling all around; but spirited troops would choose a
charge every time rather than such imbecile business as that
midnight tree-cutting exploit.

When the Confederate army was driven from Missionary
Ridge, Longstreet was compelled to raise the siege of
Knoxville. He retired to the eastward, taking position on the
East Tennessee and Virginia railroad, near Morristown, if I
remember correctly, the cavalry guarding his front.

The cold was intense. The people, in sympathy with the
enemy, furnished them with excellent guides to any exposed
position of ours. Hence we had to be exceedingly vigilant.
Imagine going on picket at 2 a.m. with temperature at zero
or below; but the army must sleep, and the cavalry must
guard the outposts. We had also numerous skirmishes, but
I can not remember the details of them.

A letter written by me to my parents dated January 4,
1864, enumerates six fights during November and December
in which the regiment lost twenty-seven killed and wounded;
one on the road to Cumberland Gap. This was early in
November. We chased some cavalry several miles, taking a
dozen or more prisoners and wounding a few without a single
casualty on our side, unless someone's ears were frost
bitten, for it was a very cold morning and a biting wind raged.

We had three or four skirmishes near Mossy creek. In

one of these, on December 26, 1863, Captain G.W. Littlefield was badly wounded by a large fragment of a shell which lacerated his left hip for a space five or six inches by twelve or thirteen. It looked like a mortal hurt. A strong constitution pulled him through, yet he was compelled to retire from the service, and even now (1911) suffers from the wound.

On the 29th of December we were ordered to drive a force of the enemy who were dismounted and lying behind a large brick residence and the outbuildings. We had to break down the garden fence, which we did by forcing our horses against it. We drove them all right, took a few prisoners, but sustained serious losses ourselves. In Company D, N.J. Allen was killed outright. Richard Berger was shot through the face, losing the sight of one eye, and William Nicholson had a slight scalp wound. There was another on the 24th, near the same place, and one near Dandridge, but I am unable to recall the incidents, although the letter referred to says that I participated in all of them. In all we sustained serious loss, and so far as I can see without any appreciable effect on the campaign; but as Forrest said, "War means fight, and fight means kill." Besides our blood was up and life held cheaply.

One little engagement, all one-sided, and as far as we were concerned, was more amusing than serious. Our brigade under Colonel Harrison, and an Alabama brigade commanded by General John T. Morgan, so long a Senator from Alabama after the war, were out on separate roads which, however, came together some distance in the rear of our position. The Alabama brigade, attacked by the enemy, gave way. We were called back, and when we reached the junction of the roads the enemy was passing in hot pursuit. In columns of fours we took them in flank, killed a few, took several prisoners and scattered the remainder, for they were so completely surprised that they made no resistance. They were Brownlow's brigade of East Tennessee Cavalry and rather shabby soldiers. We had no casualties.

The service was very arduous; besides the picketing alluded to above, foraging became very laborious. The country along the streams is quite fertile and produced abundantly of food for man and beast, but cavalry troops consume rapidly, and the valleys were soon exhausted. So we had to go away out into the mountains for supplies. Often wagons could not go the roads and we had to bring supplies on our horses over mountain trails for ten or fifteen miles. These expeditions were not without danger, for these rude mountaineers were good shots, and lying in the woods, did not see their bread and meat taken with kind feelings. They sometimes fired on these foraging parties, but at long range from mountain crag or other secure position, and I believe injured no one.

As I am not relating these things in chronological order, this will be a good place to set down the facts concerning the night alarm on the banks of Pigeon river. We were in camp for several days on the banks of this stream which, though small to be called a river, was yet rather deep at that place; though it could be forded, as will be seen.

Across from our encampment, some two or three hundred yards from the banks, was a stately mansion, the home of a wealthy and refined family. I think the people's name was Smith, but I am not sure. The name will do anyhow. The head of the family, a general or colonel, was away from home, with the army no doubt. The family at the house consisted of the mother and three or four daughters, all charming ladies. They had secured a house guard to protect them from insult. Joe Rogers, being a little indisposed, was duly installed as guard. This meant good times for Joe; a bed to sleep in, three meals a day with plate, knife and fork, a stable for his black horse Nig, of which, by the way, he was very fond.

It was not long before the society men of the regiment acquired the habit of slipping out after evening roll call to enjoy a game of cards at General Smith's. One night several of them, a lieutenant, a clerk of the quartermaster's department, and one or two others, crossed the river in a small skiff and were soon pleasantly engaged in the fascinating game of euchre with the young ladies. Suddenly there was a cry of "Halt! Halt!" and pistol shots rang out on the night air. Out went the lights, and the visitors rushed for doors and windows, knocking over chairs, tables, and even the young women. They rushed to the river, plunged in and across, and made for their companies. The first alarm was plainly heard in the camp. Sharp orders to "saddle up" were given and repeated from company to company, and the brigade was soon in line. Colonel Harrison sent Tom Gill and a small party to ascertain the cause of the row. Tom passed General Smith's, where all was dark, and went on to the picket stand. Pickets reported all quiet; no enemy had passed their post. Tom returned to the house, where he met Joe Rogers. It appeared that Joe had not run with the others at the first alarm. He had gone out the back way to look after Nig and his equipment. While getting these he heard voices, accompanied with laughter, and the voices seemed somewhat familiar. Peeping around the house he soon ascertained that the alarm had been caused by three or four Rangers. He reported the cause of the disturbance to Gill and his scouting party, and Gill reported it to Colonel Harrison.

"The old man" was furious at first, for a false alarm in war is a serious matter and a grave offense. However, after some reflection, he concluded to drop the matter, as he thought the incident would have a wholesome effect on the guilty parties. The men did not so easily let it drop. Frequently at night for some months afterwards someone would call out:

"Who waded Pigeon?

From some other part of the camp the answer would come:

"Murray! Brownson!"

The story got into the comic papers and caused some amusement and some mortification to the victims of the joke. John Haynie, one of the best soldiers of the regiment, was the leader of the alarmist jokers. If I ever learned the names of the others I have forgotten them.

We had now been in the service for considerably over two years, and there had been no general system of furloughs. Our regiment might have fifteen if they would re-enlist, but as we had already enlisted for the war we could hardly perform this condition. However, it was demanded that we make declaration of our intention to continue in the service. Some of us considered this a reflection on our honor, and decided to do without the coveted furloughs. Then some of the boys got together, made a speech or two, passed a preamble and resolutions, declaring we would never—no never—quit as long as an armed foe trod our sacred soil. This was considered satisfactory at headquarters, and the furloughs were ordered. Lots were drawn for the three assigned to Company D. These fell to D.S. Combs, I.V. Jones and J.F. McGuire, who left at once to visit their homes.

At that time the enemy was at the mouth of the Rio Grande. They evidently intended to invade the country far enough to break up a most profitable trade between the States west of the Mississippi and the outside world by way of Mexico. This traffic was carried on by means of wagons, hundreds of which went in a constant stream to the Rio Grande, loaded with cotton, and brought back supplies of all kinds. The people feared the enemy would penetrate the interior, as the State had been stripped of its defenders. Every persuasion was used to prevail on these men to remain on this side, and they finally agreed to stay. The lieutenant general commanding the department readily agreed to the arrangement, and thus Company D lost three good soldiers. We could not blame them, for, given the opportunity, every one of us perhaps would have done the same thing.

It was during this winter that one of the saddest events of all our career happened; the hanging of E.S. Dodd by the enemy. He was a member of Company D. He was of a good family and well educated. For many years he kept a diary, setting down at night the happenings of the day. He was taken prisoner with this diary in his pocket. On that evidence alone he was condemned and executed as a spy.

Spring was now approaching. Those masters of the art of war—Grant and Sherman—were preparing to strike the final blows at the tottering Confederacy. Longstreet went to Virginia. Our cavalry went to Georgia to our old commander, General Joseph Wheeler. Our way was up the French Broad river, through western North Carolina and South Carolina, marching leisurely where there were abundant supplies. We reached Georgia as Sherman was preparing to move. On the 9th day of May, just north of Dalton, we were ordered to charge a force of the enemy, which proved to be our old acquaintance, La Grange's brigade of Indiana cavalry. We went at them in our usual style, at top speed, every fellow yelling as loud as he could. They broke and retreated precipitately. We took more than sixty prisoners, including the brigade commander, Colonel La Grange. His horse was wounded and fell, pinning his rider to the earth just at a large farm gate. John Haynie, quick as a flash, was at his side, securing the prisoner, evidently an officer. Addressing his captor, the prisoner said:

"You have a prize indeed. I am Colonel La Grange. I did not know that you boys had got down here from East Tennessee. I knew you as soon as I saw you coming."

With the help of some of the prisoners he was released from his fallen horse, mounted on another, and escorted by his captor to Colonel Harrison. This incident came under my own observation. For the interview which followed his presentation to Harrison I am indebted to that officer himself, who related it to me several years after the war. La Grange said:

>"I was in command of the brigade, and was anxious for the commission of brigadier general. Had some influential friends who were helping me. My division commander told me to go out, run in the rebel pickets, skirmish a little and send in a report, which he would forward with strong recommendations for my promotion. I came out, ran into the Texas Rangers, and am a prisoner."

"Only the fortune of war, my young friend," said Harrison. "Only the fortune of war."

Our loss was quite heavy. Among the killed was Charles T. Pelham of Company D, an educated young man, of good family and fine promise, a civil engineer by profession; D.F. Lily, a young lawyer, who fell almost in sight of his mother's home, and W.H. Bigelow, a native of Canada; both of these last were of Company G, and both educated gentlemen.

CHAPTER XII.

SHERMAN'S WAGON TRAIN AND THE AFFAIRS WITH M'COOK AND STONEMAN.

The enemy, over one hundred thousand strong, under one of the ablest commanders in the Federal army, advanced on all the roads, overlapping the Confederates, who took position after position, to be turned by the superior numbers of their adversaries.

At Resaca there was quite a spirited engagement with a part of the advance. At Cassville we took position and offered battle, but retired before the flanking movement of the enemy. Near this place Wheeler turned their left and captured a train of wagons within a few miles of Sherman's army. The Rangers were not in this capture, but when the enemy sent a force of cavalry to retake his train, we met it in the most unique engagement of the war. Sherman's great army with its hundreds of cannon, thousands of wagons and other vehicles had passed along, pulverizing the roads and fields into fine dust, which covered everything, in many places several inches deep. A single horseman riding along raised a cloud, a company or regiment, such a dense fog as to obscure everything. We were in line on one side of a slight rise in the land. The cavalry of the enemy above mentioned were approaching on the other side of the hill. We were ordered forward, and at the top of this hill we met each other, enveloped in clouds of dust. We raised the usual yell, although in doing so we took in large quantities of Georgia real estate. We emptied our pistols into the dust, and the enemy broke. We did not pursue them very far; for we knew we were near their main army, and feared we might run into a brigade or two of infantry, as we could not see anything twenty feet away. Previous encounters had given us a contempt for their cavalry and we did not hesitate to charge a whole brigade if need be; but we had a wholesome respect for large bodies of infantry. We took a few prisoners, but did not know, owing to the dust, what other casualties were inflicted on them. We had seven wounded, including George Burke of Company D, who was shot in the shoulder.

Wheeler was determined to save his train, so he tried to march all night, but a violent electrical storm came up, rain fell in torrents, and our progress was very slow, for the drivers of the teams could not see the road, except by the glare of the lightning. After this had gone on for several hours, making scarcely so many miles, the command camped in column—I believe without orders.

Wheeler dearly loved their wagon trains. I believe it is safe to say that from the first to the last he captured as many wagons as he commanded men. Thousands were burned, but other thousands were secured for the use of our army. The Northern contractors probably enjoyed this as much as Wheeler; no doubt they would have been glad to replace all the wagons, for a reasonable consideration.

The retreat of the army continued to the very gates of Atlanta. Here the Rangers made another charge, in which Jesse Billingsly of Company D was killed.

During the last week of July the enemy undertook to play our game, and simultaneously made two raids on our communications. One column under General McCook, with 3500 cavalry, turned our left. They crossed the Chattahoochie near Campbelltown, passed through Fayetteville, where they burned between fifty and one hundred wagons, and struck the Macon railroad near Jonesboro, twenty or twenty-five miles below Atlanta. As soon as intelligence of this movement reached Wheeler he started for the raiders. We rode all night, coming up with them about daylight. They made very feeble resistance and we ran over them. It was now a chase of twenty miles to the Chattahoochie again. As this stream was not fordable, they made a stand to gain time for crossing the river, which they were attempting by means of boats. Our column was strung out for several miles, Harrison's brigade in front. We were dismounted and pushed into the thick woods. It was afternoon of the first day of August, and about as hot as such days ever get. The enemy made some resistance, but we drove them steadily some four or five hundred yards, when we heard firing in our rear where we had left our horses. So we had to face about and fight our way back. We got mixed up with Ross' brigade, which had been dismounted as soon as it came up. After some three hours of this work, the enemy surrendered: that is, all who had not crossed the river.

Wheeler reported 950 prisoners, 1200 horses and two pieces of artillery as the fruits of this engagement. There were many of their killed and wounded lying in the bushes. I have no information as to the number. Our regiment lost two killed and ten wounded, including one from Company D. This was V. Catron, who was shot in the leg.

The other column of the enemy, led by General Stoneman, turned our flank and struck our communications lower down, near Macon. His force was reported to be 3000. General Iverson of the Confederate cavalry attacked them and took 600 prisoners, including Stoneman himself, with two pieces of artillery. The remainder of their force in small detachments made their way back as best they could. Iverson did not have force enough to pursue them.

General Shoupe of General Hood's staff recorded in his diary, that the "First of August deserved to be marked with a white stone." These operations cost the enemy nearly half of the two raiding parties, and fully justified General Hood in saying that our cavalry were equal to twice their number of the enemy.

CHAPTER XIII.

WHEELER'S SECOND RAID INTO TENNESSEE.

Wheeler was now ordered to operate on the long line of the enemy's communications. Finding the posts and bridges south of Chattanooga too strongly fortified to offer any promise of successful attack, Wheeler determined to go over into middle Tennessee again. He went up along the Holston above Knoxville, and then had to cross under a severe fire of the enemy's pickets. For this undertaking there was a call for volunteers. It looked as if the whole of the Rangers were volunteering, and Wheeler had to stop them. The fording was deep, but the enemy were easily driven from their position. A small force, not of the Rangers, was sent down toward Knoxville. They met the enemy and were roughly handled; about half of them were taken prisoners, and the exultant enemy came on at a furious rate. Our regiment was formed in an open field. Colonel Harrison took position in front. We went forward in a walk at first, and then in a trot. The men were impatient. Officers kept saying:

"Steady, men! Keep back there!"

Then we heard the popping of pistols, and all eyes were turned on Harrison. The routed Confederates came into view. Next the enemy in close pursuit. The men could now hardly be restrained. Finally Harrison shouted:

"Well, go then! —- you, go!"

The tap of the drum on the race track never sent jockeys and racers to the front more impetuously than the Rangers went at the sound of these words. The enemy's force was small, and they faced about at once. Their horses were nearly exhausted, and we soon overtook them, capturing nearly the whole party, which did not exceed two companies.

Our march was now across the Cumberland mountains, by McMinnville, the familiar route we had traveled two years before under Forrest, and one year before under Wheeler. Just before reaching Murfreesboro we turned to the left and began to destroy the railroad leading to Chattanooga, over which Sherman's supplies had to be carried. We piled fence rails on the track and set them on fire. The heat caused the rails to expand and bend into all shapes, rendering them useless until straightened out; of course the ties were burned also. In this way we destroyed some fifty miles of the road; but the enemy had unlimited resources, and kept trains loaded with railroad material at Nashville and Louisville; these were rushed to the scene of our operations. With large forces working day and night they soon got the tracks in order.

We now moved forward to the Mussel Shoals, where we were to cross the Tennessee river. In a little skirmish on the north side W.H. Caldwell of Company D was wounded in the hip. He was disabled for the remainder of the war by this hurt; never entirely recovered, in fact, walking with a limp for the rest of his life.

After crossing the river the men of the Third Arkansas, who had shown courage and devotion on many fields, became greatly demoralized. Finding themselves nearer home than they had been for years, many of them deserted. One morning it was reported that twelve of these men had gone. A detail of twenty Rangers under Lieutenant Joiner, the whole under Captain Bass of the Third Arkansas, was sent after the deserters. I was one of this detail. Riding forty or fifty miles a day, we overtook four of them about twenty miles from the great Mississippi and made them prisoners. On the return my horse was badly injured by falling through a broken plank in an old bridge, and I was left afoot. Joiner gave me orders to remain until my horse recovered, or until I could procure another, and then join some other command until I could get company over Sand mountain, as that region was infested with bushwhackers and murderers. It was some weeks before I could get a mount, for horses were very scarce, but this is not a narrative of my operations.

Henry W. Graber joined Company B in September 1861. He was wounded near Franklin, Kentucky, captured during his recuperation in April 1863, and sent to prison at Camp Chase, Ohio, and then to Point Lookout, Maryland. He was exchanged in March 1864, rejoined his company and served until the end to the conflict. He published his memoirs of service with the Terry Rangers in 1916.

Plate 8

CHAPTER XIV.

"THE ROME RACES."

I am indebted to Comrade A.B. Briscoe for a description of this incident.

"General Harrison, our old colonel, was in command of the forces composed of ours and Ashby's brigade of mounted infantry and a battery of four guns. For some reason, but contrary to all former usages, our regiment was dismounted and placed near the battery, and Ashby's infantry kept mounted to protect the flanks and led horses. The fight had barely commenced when it was realized from the immense bodies of infantry in our front that it was a bad one. The battery was ordered to the rear, but just as they were limbered the Yankee cavalry poured in on our flanks and completely enveloped us. I did not give an order to run nor did I hear an order of any kind, but I soon found myself dodging through and among the Yankee cavalry, who were shouting to us to surrender. We reached our horses, which were not over 150 yards in the rear, mounted, and after a very hasty formation charged out through the enemy, and although we made repeated rallies they ran us back about five miles. Why the Yankees did not capture more of our men is a mystery, as outside of the battery we lost very few prisoners. To give any appropriate

name to this battle we called it 'Rome Races,' for
such it was."

In this race the colors furled around the staff and in the
oilcloth were lost—not captured—as the subjoined letter
shows:

"Dallas, Texas, May 18, 1898.
"Terry's Texas Rangers Association, Austin, Texas.

"Gentlemen: I have been in Texas since 1890,
and have frequently endeavored to find some
members of Terry's Texas Rangers, and finally, by
accident, met with your comrade, H.W. Graber,
and reported to him the finding of your flag the day
after our engagement with your forces near Rome,
Georgia. It happened in this way: I was directed by
the general commanding to take two companies
and move through the woods on the right of our
line to a certain point where a country road inter-
sected the main river road then occupied by our
brigade. Just before coming into the main road I
picked up a package or roll of something, threw it
over my saddle, and on my return to the main
command examined the same and found it to be
the Terry's Rangers' flag in its case. It seemed to
have slipped off the staff and been lost in that way.
At the suggestion of your comrade—Graber—I
have made a request on the authorities of the State
of Indiana, who have had charge of it ever since,
soon after its capture, and herewith enclose you a
letter from Chas. E. Wilson, military secretary at
Indianapolis, which seems to indicate there is no
authority with the executive department of the
State to return the flag, as it is in absolute control
of the State Legislature, which is a matter of
exceeding regret to me, as I should like to have
returned the flag to you in time for your next
reunion at Austin. I am furthermore able to assure
you that this flag was never displayed in the streets

of Nashville, as has been reported, but remained in possession of our regiment until soon after it was found. We returned direct to Louisville, from which point it was sent by express direct to the State of Indiana.

"In view of the existing unsettled condition of the country, I would suggest we let the matter rest until our country is again pacified and returned to its normal condition, when I will take pleasure in making a further effort to return this flag, which was not captured, but found, and I consider, therefore, property should be returned to its owner.

"With kind regards and best wishes, hoping to have the pleasure of a personal meeting with our association, I am, with great respect,

"Yours very truly,

"J.J. Wiler,

"Maj. Com. 17th Indiana Volunteer Infantry."

This flag was returned to the survivors at Dallas in October, 1898. Its loss was very mortifying to the Rangers, as it had been presented shortly before by the ladies of middle Tennessee.

In justice to the knightly "Count" Jones, I must say that no one could have taken the colors from him without taking his life.

In this action fell Wm. Nicholson of Company D and Lieutenant Batchelor of Company C, and perhaps others, but I have no record of them.

The last known Regimental flag of the Terry Texas Rangers, presented to them in September 1864 but lost a month later unrolled in its rubber covering during a skirmish at Coosaville, Georgia. The flag was returned to the Rangers by the Governor of the State of Indiana in October 1899 and is now in the possession of the Texas Division, United Daughters of the Confederacy. The flag measures approximately 28" x 43". The field is dark blue with a white center circle. The cross is red with yellow stars and the lettering is dark blue.
Plate 9

CHAPTER XV.

THE LAST CAMPAIGN.

Wheeler's cavalry was now almost the only obstacle to Sherman's great march to the sea. They harassed his columns front, flanks and rear, picking up many prisoners; but three or four thousand cavalry could make little resistance to the onward sweep of 60,000 veterans under one of the greatest captains of modern times. Conflicts were of almost daily occurrence. The Rangers were engaged at Buckhead Church and Waynesboro, Georgia. Again at Aiken, South Carolina. At Averysboro and Fayetteville, North Carolina, where, after a night's march, they surprised Kilpatrick's cavalry camp, but failed to bag that redoubtable leader. In all of these conflicts the losses were heavy. Old Company D lost in killed, John Gage, P.R. Kennedy, Dave Nunn, Sam Screws and Jim Wynne. Their list of wounded, too, was large. P.R. Kyle and Geo. T. McGehee, good ones both, were badly hurt at Aiken; McArthur, Brannum and P.J. Watkins also. The other companies sustained heavy losses. Lieutenant Heiskell of Company K was killed. I wish I could name them all.

In all of these actions, the remnant of nearly 1200 enlistments charged with that dauntless courage which had characterized them at Woodsonville, at Bardstown, at Dalton and many other brilliant fields of arms. Their old colonel, now a brigadier general, Thomas Harrison; their colonel, the knightly Cook, and the staid and ever reliable Major Jarmon, were all stretched on beds, racked with the pains of severe wounds. The command now devolved on Captain Matthews, who but a little over a year before had been elected lieutenant, promoted to the rank of captain by the bullets of the enemy which brought down his superiors, was now, at Bentonville, to lead the old regiment in the last charge, which will always rank as one of the most brilliant feats of arms in the history of wars. As I was not present I will let Lieutenant Briscoe tell of it, for he tells it well.

THE LAST CHARGE.

"We did but little fighting the first day, as the enemy changed positions very rapidly. But the second we were engaged in some severe skirmishes all the forenoon, in one of which Major Jarmon, our only remaining field officer, was severely wounded, when we were withdrawn a few hundred yards to rest and give place for the infantry.

"We had been in this position resting and eating our rations probably over an hour, when we heard the boom of artillery directly in our rear. Every man pricked up his ears, for we knew that it meant something serious. Captain Doc Matthews of Company K (my company) was in command of the regiment, which numbered about 100 men. We were standing talking of the probable cause of the artillery fire in our rear when General Wheeler galloped up and asked for the commander of the Rangers. He seemed a little excited. His order was, 'Captain, mount your men, go as fast as you can and charge whatever you find at the bridge.' These were almost his exact words. In less time than it takes to tell it, we were mounted and racing to the rear. Within about a half a mile of the bridge we passed a small brigade of infantry 'double quicking' in the same direction. We saluted each other with a cheer as we passed, for all felt that it was a critical time in the battle. As we came upon some rising ground we had a good view of the enemy across an open field about 500 yards distant. Here we halted an instant to close up the column, and for Captain Matthews to salute General Hardee and staff, who wished to know what troops we were.

"Captain Matthews told him and of our orders from General Wheeler. He took a look across the field at the dense blue line and said, 'Then execute your orders.' It looked like the old regiment was this time surely going to its grave. Everything was so plain and clear you could see the men handling their guns and hear their shouts of command. Without a moment's hesitation Captain Matthews gave the order, 'Charge right in front,' and with that wonderful rebel yell we charged across the 500 yards of open field upon and among the mass of Yankees. We rode them down and emptied our pistols at close range. When the force of the charge was expended we fell back with about 200 prisoners."

Like our other brilliant charges, it was the very audacity that brought success.

In this charge fell, mortally wounded, Wm. J. Hardee, Jr., son of Lieutenant General Hardee. Nearly a year before he, with several other boys, had run away from school to join the Rangers, but on account of their extreme youth Colonel Harrison sent them back to school. The boy would not remain in school, so General Hardee kept him with him for several month[s], but he fretted to join the Rangers. Finally the father consented. The boy was enlisted in Company D and fell in this, his first action.

I reached the command shortly before the surrender. The regiment in numbers was little more than a good company. Battle and disease had claimed and received their toll; but this little remnant seemed as full of courage and spirit as when first they left their State.

The dream was over. General Lee, "yielding to overwhelming numbers and resources," had laid down his arms. General Johnston, again in command of the Army of Tennessee, agreed with Sherman to disband his army. Sadly the Rangers dispersed, taking the roads to their distant homes.

General Wheeler issued the following order, which for intense feeling and felicity of expression is a gem:

"Headquarters Cavalry Corps,
"April 28, 1865.

"Gallant Comrades: You fought your fight. Your task is done. During a four years' struggle for liberty you have exhibited courage, fortitude and devotion. You are the victors of more than 200 sternly contested fields. You have participated in more than a thousand conflicts of arms. You are heroes! Veterans! Patriots! The bones of your comrades mark battlefields upon the soil of Kentucky, Virginia, North Carolina, South Carolina, Georgia, Alabama and Mississippi. You have done all that human exertion could accomplish. In bidding you adieu, I desire to tender my thanks for your gallantry in battle, your fortitude under suffering and your devotion at all times to the holy cause you have done so much to maintain. I desire also to express my gratitude for the kind feelings you have seen fit to extend toward myself, and to invoke upon you the blessing of our Heavenly Father, to whom we must always look in the hour of distress.

Brethren, in the cause of freedom, comrades in arms, I bid you farewell.

"Joseph Wheeler,

"Major General.

"Official:

"Wm. E. Waites,

"Assistant Adjutant General."

Bentonville, North Carolina, the morning after the battle. The smoke is from resin that was fired by the Confederates. Plate 10

*Gustave Cooke enlisted in Company H in 1861, was elected
sergeant, and eventually rose through the ranks to command the
regiment in late 1864. He was wounded several times, most
severely at the battle of Bentonville in March 1865. His long
recovery left him unable to return to Texas until December 1865.*
Plate 11

CHAPTER XVI.

CONCLUSION.

I am well aware of the imperfections of this work. I can only say that I have tried to tell an unvarnished tale, to do no one injustice, nothing extenuate nor set down aught in malice. Beyond a few old letters which have escaped the ravages of mice, and such official reports as I could find, I have been compelled to rely on memory—frail and unreliable at best, more so after the lapse of half a century. I beg to remind those who may find fault that it is much easier to find fault than to do good work. No two persons see events exactly alike. This is illustrated in our courts every day.

From the standpoint of the martinet our organization could hardly be called a regiment. A distinguished lieutenant general is reported as saying that it was not a regiment at all but "a d — d armed mob." If there was ever any serious attempt to discipline it the effort was soon abandoned. Volunteers we began, volunteers we remained to the end. If any wished to evade duty, they found a way, and the punishment for evasion was light. To our credit it may be said that few ever avoided a fight. There were few real cowards among us, and they were simply objects of pity. If a man did not wish to go into a fight he held his horse until it was over.

One reason of our almost uniform success was the superiority of our arms. It will be remembered that at the beginning the possession of a good pistol was a requisite for enlistment. If a man died or was killed his comrades kept his pistol. When a prisoner of the enemy's cavalry was taken this part of his outfit was added to the general stock, so that after a few months most, if not all, had two weapons of this kind, and some even tried to carry three or four. No other regiment of the army was so supplied.

Again, it was a noteworthy fact that the men were all good horsemen, accustomed to the use and management of horses from childhood. When three or four hundred of such men, charging as fast as their horses would go, yelling like Comanches, each delivering twelve shots with great rapidity and reasonable accuracy, burst into the ranks of an enemy, the enemy generally gave way. It did not take us long to find this out; also the enemy were not slow to "catch on."

If it be said that other commands lost more men in battle, the explanation is simple and easy. The purpose of fighting is to destroy the enemy in battle; all drill, organization and hard marches are to this end—to kill and wound as many of the enemy as possible. If this is granted, the Rangers invite comparison with the best in any army. It is safe to claim that the regiment killed, wounded and captured a number of the enemy at least several times our highest enlistment of nearly 1200. If it be said that my claim for superiority is biased by prejudice in favor of my own regiment, I will give estimates of others.

In a letter to me acknowledging an invitation to one of our reunions, General Wheeler said:

"They were unceasingly vigilant, matchlessly brave and daring."

General Thomas Jordan, an educated soldier, a writer of ability, chief of staff to General Beauregard, was selected by Forrest and his principal officers to write a history of the campaigns of that great soldier. In a note on page 160 of his book, General Jordan says:

"This regiment was raised and commanded by the lamented Colonel Terry, whose brief military career, beginning as a volunteer scout at the first Manassas, was full of distinction. He was killed at Woodsonville, Kentucky. The privates included a large number of the wealthiest and best educated young men of Texas, who, with many others specially trained in the business of stock raising on the vast prairies of that State, had acquired a marvelous skill in horsemanship. The career of this regiment has been one of the most brilliant in the annals of war."

Dr. John A. Wyeth, who also wrote a life of Forrest, says, "No braver men ever lived than the Texas Rangers."

General Hood ("Advance and Retreat," page 202) writes of the cavalry:

"I had, moreover, become convinced that our cavalry were able to successfully compete with double their numbers. The Confederacy possessed, in my opinion, no body of cavalry superior to that which I found guarding the flanks of the Army of Tennessee when I assumed its direction."

I now quote Federal authority. Writing of the comparative merits of the soldiers of the two armies, in a paper on the Kentucky campaign, General Buell, while denying the superiority of the Southern soldiers over the Northern, admits it was true of the cavalry. He says:

"Another sectional distinction produced a more marked effect in the beginning of the war. The habits of the Southern people facilitated the formation of cavalry corps which were comparatively efficient even without instruction; and accordingly we see Stuart, John Morgan and Forrest riding with impunity around the union armies, destroying or harassing their communications. Late in the war that agency was reversed. The South was exhausted of horses, while the Northern cavalry increased in numbers and efficiency, and acquired the audacity which had characterized the South-ern."

Read that again. It comes very near saying that the South was overcome because the supply of horses failed. The writer is an educated soldier and student of war.

L'ENVOI.

My task is done. My story is told. I have derived pleasure as well as pain and grief from the recital: pleasure in going back over the dreary waste of years to the morning of life, and dwelling in memory amid the scenes of my early man-hood: pain that I can not do justice to all who, at the call of country, periled their young lives for home and the right; grief for the heroic dead, who sleep in unmarked graves wherever duty lead to danger and death. Their matchless courage and devotion earned undying fame.

"Their praise is hymned by loftier harps than mine;

Yet, one I would select from that proud throng":

Because he was my bedfellow, and I loved him as a brother; faithful in the discharge of every duty, clean, brave, and true—William Nicholson.

John Walker Hill and Robert Edward Hill. John Hill was sergeant of Company D from 1861-1865. He was taken prisoner at Murfreesboro, Tenn. December 31, 1862, imprisoned at Camp Douglas, Illinois, and exchanged in April 1863. He rejoined his company and served until the end of the war. Robert Hill first enlisted in Company D, then became Assistant Surgeon on the Regimental Staff. He was captured four times. Plate 12

George Quincy Turner
served as a private in
company C from
1861-1864. He died from
illness in Dallas County,
Alabama in March 1864.
Plate 13

Benjamin Franklin
Batchelor served as a
Lieutenant in Company C
from 1861-1864. He was
mortally wounded in a
skirmish on the Coosa
River in October 1864.
Plate 14

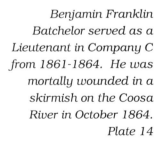

Austin Robinson was a private in Company A from 1861 until the end of the war. He was wounded at Salt River, Kentucky, in October 1862 and taken prisoner. When exchanged he rejoined his unit for the Georgia and Carolina campaigns.
Plate 15

Gabriel B. Beaumont enlisted in Company A in September 1861. He was wounded in the shoulder at the battle of Murfreesboro in December 1862 and was medically discharged shortly thereafter at the age of sixteen.
Plate 16

*Achille Ferris enlisted in Company H in March 1862 at the age of
nineteen. Shortly thereafter he posed for this wartime portrait.
Records indicate he was paroled at Demopolis, Alabama.*
Plate 17

REMINISCENCES OF THE
TERRY RANGERS

BY J.K.P. BLACKBURN

To the Blackburn family, its affinities, descendants and representatives I dedicate this small volume of personal experiences and reminiscences during the Civil War between the States, from 1861 to 1865, inclusive.

J.K.P. BLACKBURN.

Lynnville, Tenn.
This December 26, 1916.

Explanatory

At times I have been requested by my children and a few friends to write some reminiscences of the Civil War as came under my observation or related to me by fellow soldiers serving with me, at first hand, as it were. Also, to relate as best I may, when I served, where I served, why I served, in the Confederate Army.

After fifty years have gone and the activities of half a century have passed by, leaving me more or less weakened in body and mind, I have consented to jot down such things as may be indelibly fixed in my mind pertaining to that period of my life, trusting and praying that I may be able to record such things in fairness and justice to all, without prejudice against any. To this end, I would ask the blessings of the Great Author and Maker of all things.

J.K.P. Blackburn.

Captain Blackburn's reminiscences of the Civil War were transcribed from a manuscript presented by the author to his niece, Mrs. W.D. Hunter, of Austin, Texas. Originally these reminiscences were printed in *The Southwestern Historical Quarterly*, XXII, 38-77; 143-179. Dr. Charles W. Ramsdell, Professor of American History in the University of Texas, edited the volume for publication, and has contributed what annotations it was deemed necessary to add.

On February 20, 1919, Captain Blackburn, then in good health, celebrated his eighty-second birthday.

REMINISCENCES OF THE TERRY RANGERS

When the Civil War commenced I was in school in Lavaca County, Texas, both as teacher and pupil, where I had been most of the time for four and a half years before. I was born in Tennessee in 1837 and in the fall of 1856, when I was about 19 years of age, my father emigrated to Texas with his family of wife and eight children. I taught a little primary school in Fayette County first for three months. Then I sold a horse my father gave me, got my money for teaching school, put these two funds together, and went to Alma Institute in Lavaca County for two years. I taught one year in Gonzales County, and after thus adding to my bank account, returned to my *alma mater* as pupil and assistant teacher and was there until hostilities commenced between the North and the South.

My first experience in anything that looked like warfare was had in a trip to San Antonio to help capture the Federal forces and war equipage at that place. The United States had been accustomed for years to make San Antonio an army post with a good force and plenty of army supplies under able commanders so as to be available to protect the western border from invasion. Soon after the State of Texas passed the ordinance of secession, Ben McCulloch, a frontiersman and Indian fighter, called upon the people living in the western and southern counties of Texas to meet him at the earliest possible moment at a rendezvous near San Antonio with any firearms to be had. Without delay nearly all the men able to bear arms and to do military duty, started with a rush, riding continuously without rest or sleep until we reached the place of gathering, which if my memory serves me, was on Sea Willow Creek a few miles from the city to the north. We who were from Lavaca County reached the place late in the night, probably two or three o'clock a.m. McCulloch had already sent men to surround the Alamo, then used as a fort and an arsenal for army and military supplies.

The movement was made with much caution and secrecy. Men with rifles in hands were placed on top of the surrounding buildings so as to command the place the artillery men must occupy when they would attempt to fire the cannon. The headquarters of General Twiggs, one mile out in the country, were picketed by a file of armed men so as to prevent communication with his forces in town. When daylight came a flag of truce was sent in to the commander at the fort, a demand for surrender made, his attention called to men on the housetops and the forces now coming in to surround the fort and his army; and without firing a gun he surrendered everything he commanded.[1]

In the meantime General Twiggs ordered his carriage and started for camp without seemingly knowing what had happened while he slept. Two of our men met him as he started out, presented their shot guns and told him he was their prisoner of war and so they marched him into the Grand Plaza where McCulloch and his men to the number of several hundred had assembled. I happened to be standing within a few steps of McCulloch when General Twiggs was brought in and I heard their conversation. After salutations General Twiggs said, "Ben McCulloch, you have treated me most

---

[1] February 16, 1861.

shamefully, ruining my reputation as a military man and I am now too old to re-establish it." McCulloch answers, "I am serving my State, the State of Texas, Sir." General Twiggs replied, that if an old woman with a broomstick in hand had come to him and having authority from the State of Texas demanded his surrender he would have yielded without a word of protest. "But you, Sir, without papers, without any notice have assembled a mob and forced me to terms." So ends this episode. General Twiggs in his humiliation wept like a child and he had my sympathy and the sympathy I think of all who witnessed this meeting. The soldiers and arms and munitions of war captured—I cannot now recall numbers or amounts.[2]

I returned to school, but school work seemed tame and commonplace and overshadowed by the tragic events on every side. War was declared by Lincoln on the seceded States, calling for troops from the other Southern States to help put down the rebellion. The Confederate Government had been formed at Montgomery, Alabama. A blaze of enthusiasm and resentment sweeping over the southland prompted patriots on every hand to get ready to defend their homes and firesides against the ravages and destruction of an insolent foe who was then moving to invade the South. The seceded States established drill and instruction camps in different parts of their borders, training men on every hand for effectual fighting. The camps were provided with competent drill masters, mobilization went on day after day

---

[2] In the whole department of Texas 2445 officers and men were surrendered by Twiggs. See report of Colonel C.A. Waite, U.S. Army, to Lorenzo Thomas, February 26, 1861, *Official Records of the Union and Confederate Armies*, Series I, Vol. I, p. 524.

The value of the grounds, buildings and stores of all kinds surrendered in San Antonio was estimated at $781,808.39; at the other posts in Texas, $700,000. See report of the Texas Commissioners, Devine, Luckett, and Maverick. *Official Records.* Series I, Vol. LIII, p. 632.

through the spring and the early summer and on through the year, and regiments were formed and sent forward towards the seat of war until thousands upon thousands were mustered into service from every section that year, the year of 1861. I spent several weeks at Camp Clark on the San Marcos River, drilling and learning military tactics at that camp of instruction. All conversation on every side pertained to war and incidents and hopes and fears connected therewith. The question of, "Are you going to the war?" was rarely asked, but "Where will you go?"

I had a room-mate the last session in school named Foley large hearted, intellectual and a poet, a Baptist preacher of ability, and a native of New York City. He and I discussed the question often and while we both preferred cavalry service, being good horsemen, he preferred to go west and northwest with the first regiment formed, I to go towards the east in order to be upon the main fields of battle even if I had to go with the infantry. We separated. He enlisted in Colonel Ford's Second Texas Cavalry and went to meet the enemy that was threatening Texas from the northwest. The next news I had from that Command, Foley had been killed in a charge on a battery at Valverda or Glorietta, New Mexico, (I have forgotten which)—killed by the last shot fired from that battery before its capture. Thus passed from earth one of the noblest spirits I ever knew.

I considered a proposition from Captain Fly who was raising a company in our neighborhood for the 2nd Texas Infantry and at one time told him I thought I might join his company when they got ready to start, but told him of my preference for the cavalry. Weeks passed. At last the opportunity came. A regiment of cavalry was to be raised in western and southern Texas for service in Virginia. Two Texans of wealth and leisure, B.F. Terry, a sugar planter, and Thos. S. Lubbock, a lawyer, who were traveling in the East—whether for business, pleasure, or curiosity, I know not—happened at or purposely were at the battle of first Manassas in Virginia, and rendered all the aid they could to the Southern cause. Terry acted as volunteer aid to the commanding general, and Lubbock also exposed his life in bearing messages during the contest. About the middle of August commissions came to Terry and Lubbock from the war department at Richmond, Virginia, authorizing them to raise a regiment on certain conditions, viz.: each man to furnish his own arms (double-barrelled shotgun and two six shooters), his bridle, blanket, saddle, spurs, lariat, etc., the Government to mount the men on good horses. The men should always select their own officers from colonel down to fourth corporal and serve in the Virginia army as an independent command. This was the opportunity that many had wished for and in less than twenty days this call was answered by 1170 men assembling at Houston to be enrolled in the regiment, afterwards called Terry's Texas Rangers. Colonel Terry immediately after securing the commission selected ten men in different sections and counties of the southern and western part of the State and asked them to raise a company of about a hundred men and bring them to Houston for enrollment in the army as soon as practical.

The company which I joined was made up from Fayette, Lavaca and Colorado counties, the majority being from Fayette. L.M. Strobel, having the authority, enrolled the names and set a day for meeting at Lagrange in Fayette County for organizing the company by electing officers from captain to corporal. At the called meeting Strobel was elected captain, W.R. Jarman first lieutenant, Phocian and William Tate (brothers) were elected second and third lieutenants, C.D. Barnett orderly sergeant, and J.T.J. Culpepper second sergeant. I cannot recall with any certainty the names of the other noncommissioned officers at this date. Our next meeting was called for Houston, Texas, where we were to be sworn in as soldiers of the Confederate States. Early in September the city of Houston was filled with volunteers anxious to enlist in the Terry Rangers. One thousand men were expected to constitute the regiment, but more and more were enlisted until the number reached 1170, an average of 117 to each company, and others, I don't recall how many, were denied the privilege of enlistment.

A Lieutenant Sparks, who had belonged to the United States army if I mistake not, came authorized to administer the oath of allegiance to the Confederate States and enroll us as her soldiers. A little incident happened at the time which showed the feelings and determination of the men. They were lined up on three sides of a hollow square (as I now remember). The enrolling officer in the center asked this question, "Do you men wish to be sworn into service for twelve months or for three years or for during the war?" With a unanimity never surpassed, a shout unheard of before, that whole body of men shouted, "For the war," "For the war!" not one expecting or caring to return until the war was over, long or short, and the invaders had been driven from our borders.

And now the regiment is ready for service, as fine a body as ever mustered for warfare. The majority of them were college boys, and cowboys, professional men, men with finished education, men just out of college, others still under-graduates, men raised in the saddles, as it were, experts with lariat and with six shooters, and not a few from the farm, from the counting houses and from shops. Just why the regiment did not elect field officers and become a fully organized body of soldiers at Houston I never knew. In the absence of this organization, the companies not being numbered or lettered, each company was called by its captain's name. Ours was Captain Strobel's company, and was sent forward as the vanguard of the regiment toward the seat of war by Colonel Terry who assumed command although he refused to be called Colonel until he should be elected to the position by his men. The election took place in Kentucky in December following.

The company was put in box freight cars and started eastward over what was afterwards to be called the Sunset Route, which at that time ran east from Eagle Lake, Colorado County, Texas, through the city of Houston, to New Iberia, Louisiana.[3] Our baggage and guns were put in the cars with us, each man retaining and wearing his pistols as regularly as his clothes. At New Iberia was a gap[4] where the road had not been built reaching to Brashear City, Louisiana, about 100 miles. Over this gap we were supposed to walk and most of the company without a murmur commenced this march. The captain had hired wagons to transport the baggage and guns. A few men found horses they could hire for the trip and so we started with eight or ten men riding horseback and the balance on foot. The country was level, for the most part, the road was good, but innumerable lagoons or sloughs lay across this roadway from six inches to two feet deep and there was no way to cross them except to wade them. With this kind of experience, a half day found most of the men with blistered sore feet, and the further we went the more aggravated was their condition. So the captain, who was

---

[3] Mr. Blackburn's memory is slightly at fault here. The railroads ran from Alleyton on the Colorado, a few miles northwest of Eagle Lake, to Harrisburg, and from Houston to Beaumont, though the track of this latter road was laid to Orange. See *Atlas of Official Records*, Plate CLVII; also A.M. Gentry to Secretary of War, Richmond, May 1, 1861, *Official Records*, Series IV, Vol.I, p. 1109.

[4] This gap in the railroad ran from Orange through New Iberia to Brashear City. L.B. Giles, Terry's Texas Rangers, pp. 15-16, says: "From Houston to Beaumont, over a newly constructed railroad, it took nearly all day to make eighty miles. From Beaumont, by steamboat down the Neches and up the Sabine to Niblett's Bluff; thence a hundred miles on foot, through water much of the way; thence forty miles in carts. . . . At New Iberia, on Bayou Teche, we were transferred to boats, and went down between the beautiful banks of that stream to Brashear, now Morgan City."

mounted, decided by the middle of the afternoon he would mount his men by impressing horses for the balance of the journey. That section was full of horses running in great herds on its prairies, so he and his mounted men found a herd of more than 100 head of all ages, sorts, and sizes, and penned them on or near the road while his baggage wagons were halted at little streams nearby. When the footmen reached the place they were told to look up their baggage, take their lariats, go to the pen and mount themselves, and the evening might be spent in breaking their horses and getting ready for the march next day.

The ages of the horses were from three to eight years, many of them had never been haltered before, some few were broken and gentle, and some of the older ones had been handled some but spoiled in attempting to break them and turned out on the range to go free. Of this last class I got one, an eight year old, Claybank gelding; but whatever their condition or habits, they were all well broken by dark that night. Next morning one of my mess-mates, Patton by name, a school and classmate for several years, found his horse was loose and gone and could not be found anywhere near. The company was preparing to move. I went to the captain, explained the situation and asked permission to return to that pen and get another horse for Patton. He consented. Another one of my mess-mates told me he had been lucky enough to get a horse fairly well broken and gentle and that he would exchange with me until I went on that errand and returned. The company moved off and Patton was left at camp alone to await my coming with his horse. I rode back about six hundred yards to the pen where we had corraled the horses that evening. It was empty and I inquired at the house nearby of ladies—no men being at home—for the horses. They told me they had been turned out into a very large grass pasture nearby lying out south of the house. I went into that pasture and rode south from the residence;

but concerning what happened for the balance of that day I am indebted to those good ladies for the information, for my mind suddenly became blank as to that matter and never since that time to this good day have I been able to recall anything that happened after I started south from the house that day. About sunset I revived enough to realize that some one was sitting by me, pouring cold water on my head and I asked in surprise, "What do mean by this treatment?" and "Where am I?" Patton answered, "You have been dead all day and I am trying this treatment to revive you." He then told me he had waited for me at the camp until he became uneasy at my failure to return and came up to this house hunting for me and found me there in an unconscious condition. Then the kind hearted ladies told me that I had early in the morning gone out into their pasture and had driven up a bunch of horses near the house, made a dash at them and had lassoed one of them and being unable to manage the animal I was riding, the lassoed animal made a quick circuit around me, jerked me off on the ground upon my head and that they had gone out there, dragged me to the house in an unconscious condition. They further stated the two horses thus lashed together by the lariat around the horn of my saddle on one and around the neck of the other ran off at a furious pace to overtake those gone on before, ran one on each side of the same tree, bringing on a collision resulting in the death of the one and the fatal wounding of the other. The ladies had also brought my saddle, blanket and lariat to the house.

Now night had come on. Our company was a day's journey ahead of us and we two soldiers were left to shift for our transportation the best we could. We consulted about what was best to be done. Patton had learned the family possessed two carriage horses in their barn and we paid the ladies $5.00 for their use to ride until we should overtake our company, pledging our honor as soon as we reached the camp to return them by their driver who was to accompany us. We saddled up and started at once, riding all night before we overtook the company. We sent back the horses with many thanks and journeyed from there to Brashear City, Patton and I in baggage wagons. At Brashear City we were all put on railroad trains again and soon after reached New Orleans, where we were quartered in a cotton compress building. Next day, aboard the cars on the Mississippi Central road we resumed our journey, without any incident of note until we reached Grand Junction, Tennessee, where we received a telegram from Colonel Terry ordering us to remain there awaiting further orders from him.

About two days later another message came announcing the fact that General Albert Sidney Johnston had interceded with the Secretary of War for our service—I mean the services of this Terry Ranger Regiment—and that we should take up our journey for Nashville, Tennessee, where General Johnston had arranged for our horses and munitions of war. This change of destination brought deep disappointment and displeasure to every one, as their hearts had been set on going to Virginia. General A.S. Johnston was a West Pointer, had served in the U.S. army both in the Mexican War and later on western frontier. He had a home and farm in Texas, and had resigned his position in the army when Texas seceded from the Union and accepted service in the Confederate army, and was at that time commanding the nucleus of what was afterwards the army of Tennessee, at Bowling Green, Kentucky. To Nashville we journeyed, and when we reached the city, encamped on the old fair grounds in West Nashville. Other companies of the regiment soon followed us and in a short time the whole regiment was encamped at Nashville.

The news of our coming and stories of the marvelous acts of horsemanship of the cowboys had preceded us; and we proved to be a great attraction for the people of Nashville and surrounding county—so much so that crowds gathered in the mornings and greater crowds in the evenings every day while we were getting in our horses in that city. Every wild, unbroken, vicious horse in that section was brought in to be ridden. When one came in there was generally a rush made by the soldiers to get first chance at him. When he had been bridled and saddled one would mount him, pull off the bridle, turn him loose, put spurs to him, and bid him do his worst. Before he was half though with the performance another soldier would spring upon him as a hind-rider and after a time, depending upon the strength of the animal, he would come to a stand-still, completely exhausted and his riders were ready for the next act.

One attraction for the spectators was the ease with which the horsemen could ride in full gallop or fast run and pick up from the ground anything they wished to. To start this performance it would be announced from the stand or some prominent place that a number of silver dollars would be strewn along on the race track for anyone that would run at full speed and pick them up. This proposition would create much rivalry and interest among those who had gotten their mounts and a half dozen, sometimes more, would enter the contest, for by this time many had exhausted their pocket change. The money was placed by the spectators along the track at intervals of twenty paces or more apart in full view of the horsemen, and at a signal all started and generally every dollar was picked up the first dash made. Well, the spectators seemed to tire of the dollar proposition in a few days and reduced the offer to half dollars which was as readily accepted and gathered as the dollars. Later on another reduction to 25c was made and still later the ladies would bring in many bouquets to be given away in the same manner, but the rivalry and interest among the performers never ceased and thus was an entertainment given from day to day that brought many thousands of spectators during the regiment's sojourn at the Fair grounds.

During the month of November, I think, there broke out in camp a great epidemic of measles of a very violent form, which was no respecter of persons seemingly, for most of the members had it, some in milder form than others, but it seemed to touch every one. To show how general it was in its attacks I quote from Henry Middlebrooks of our company. He said his mother had told him he had measles when a babe and he had measles when he was fifteen years old and he had them now so badly as to be rendered unfit for duty and was discharged from the service. Captain Strobel's company was first to lose a man from this epidemic, M.G. Harborough being the victim. The hospitals at Nashville and many private houses were filled with the sick and dying. I was sent to one of the hospitals where for weeks I was kept alive by the best of nursing and attention of the good ladies of Nashville who, in regular reliefs, nursed the sick night and day. God bless the good ladies of Nashville. They will always have a warm place in my heart, for my own mother could not have nursed me more carefully and constantly. The epidemic continued its fight upon the regiment until the middle of December, maybe a little longer. About that time I reported to the regiment for duty at a little village about fifteen miles north of Bowling Green, Kentucky, Oakland by name, where I joined about 150 men able for duty. Over 1000 men had been eliminated by measles; many of them died and others were discharged on account of disability and others still to return later on as they recovered. I can't recall numbers now, but I might safely say as many or perhaps more in our regiment died of this epidemic than were killed in battle in the four years the war continued.

An incident connected with the removal of the regiment from Nashville to Kentucky I feel should be mentioned at this time. Colonel Terry as a precaution against possible trouble had arranged for guards to be placed around the camp every night to prevent the men from going up town. The men, undisciplined as they were, looked upon this as an unnecessary restriction upon their general liberty, and so some of the most determined ones would manage to get out and go up every night and sometimes they would get unruly or noisy from drink and fall into the hands of the police and be locked up; but generally they were released after short detention and a promise of good behavior in the future. In this way there was some bad blood between the "cops" and the Texans, which soon brought on a crisis and bloodshed and death to some of the police force. One night three or four soldiers slipped by the guards, went up town, imbibed too freely of booze, went to the theater and took their seats in the gallery. Captain John Smith's expected execution and Pocahontas' rescue as related in early history of the Colonies was the drama staged for the night. When that part of the play was reached where Captain John Smith, condemned to die by his Indian captors, was bound hand and foot and his head placed upon a rock, the executioner drew back his bludgeon to strike the fatal blow, Pocahontas thrust her own body between Smith's head and the descending bludgeon, one of the boozy solders in the gallery whipped out a six-shooter and fired upon the supposed executioner with the remark that "his mother had taught him to always protect a lady when in danger." This shot missed its mark, but created consternation and stopped the play. The police rushed in to arrest the offender, the other soldiers helped him to resist arrest, and shooting began, resulting in the death of two policemen and the wounding of another one and the freedom of the solders to return unmolested to camp. This tragedy was reported to the Governor of Tennessee and immediately telegraphed by the Governor to General Johnston, who ordered Colonel Terry to come immediately on the first train to Bowling Green and report to him. By daylight next morning the regiment was in the train on their way to their destination nearer to the scenes that should soon be enacted between contending lines of battle. The baggage and the horses collected for the use of the regiment up to this time were sent on through the country by a detail of men with an officer in charge.

When Colonel Terry reported to General Johnston's headquarters, at Bowling Green, he was ordered to assemble his regiment at Oakland, fifteen miles north of Bowling Green. About the first business attended to in the new quarters was to hold an election for regimental officers and to cast lots for assignment of companies to their places in the regiment. This resulted in the election of B.F. Terry for Colonel, Thos. S. Lubbock for Lieutenant-Colonel, and Thos. Harrison for Major. Martin Royston was selected as Adjutant and W.B. Sayers as Sergeant Major. Captain Strobel's company, to which I belonged, drew the letter F for its number of place in the regiment. The other companies drew other letters of the alphabet, from A to K, inclusive, except J, and thereafter the companies were called and known by letters instead of by captains' names. The organization now being complete, a roster was made out and sent to the Secretary of War at Richmond, Virginia, and an application made for numbering the regiment, and for commissions for all commissioned officers of the same. The number assigned us was 8th Texas Cavalry, when we would have been 2nd Texas Cavalry but for the two or three months interval between our enrollment and final organization. The first duty assigned us was to patrol and picket all that section from Bowling Green north as far up as Woodsonville on Green River, Kentucky.

The winter came on with much snow and hard freezing weather. The men were coming in slowly from their sick beds. Those already in camps had to do double duty, owing to their small numbers and the great amount of the work to be done. It was not uncommon for men to be compelled to stand picket in the snow several inches deep for four hours at a time and then be relieved for two hours and be put in again for four hours. This duty was very trying on the constitutions of those just recovering from an attack of measles. This unusual experience brought bronchial troubles or affections upon me, and although it did not send me to the hospital again, yet I have never up to this day gotten entirely rid of it.

On the 17th day of December the regiment made a reconnaissance up near Woodsonville, Kentucky. The turnpike ran parallel with the railroad for some distance before we reached the village. Colonel Terry sent two companies up the railroad and the balance of the regiment kept the pike. On near approach to the village on Green River, the two companies came suddenly upon about an equal number of the enemy who were concealed behind some haystacks and a fence near the railroad, who saluted the Texans with a volley of musketry which told heavily upon them, but the Texans charged them on horseback and drove them back toward the village. In the meantime the balance of the regiment had come up on a rise or deviation in the pike in view of the conflict, several hundred yards from us to our right. We were halted there for a little while and sitting on our horses in column of twos when suddenly without the least suspicion of what was about to happen, a heavy volley of musketry was turned upon us from a black jack thicket on the hillside east of us and very close to us. Colonel Terry immediately ordered a charge, emphasizing the order with an oath not easily forgotten, so we made a rush for those bushes concealing a considerable force with bayonets fixed ready to receive us. With our shotguns loaded with buckshot we killed, wounded, and scattered that command in short order. Our casualties were comparatively few in numbers, but fearful in results, as we lost our Colonel, shot through the jaw, the bullet ranging up through the brain. He and his horse and three of the enemy fell in a heap. He had shot two and a ranger near him, I think, shot the third one.

This was the 32nd Indiana Regiment of Infantry we fought, commanded by Colonel Willich so we were informed by the prisoners we captured. This was our first battle and the first engagement of the army of Tennessee. We had ridden into an ambuscade and if the enemy had lowered their fire sufficiently in that first volley, there is no good reason why we would not all have been killed or wounded. One lesson we learned from that experience that served us well in future operations. That was to have flankers out on each side of a moving column as well as a vanguard whenever we might suspect an enemy, so as to avoid ambuscades.

In the engagement at Woodsonville Captain Walker of Company K was wounded by a bayonet passing through his lower arm and slightly wounding him in the chest. What the losses were on each side, I cannot now recall.[5]

When Colonel Terry was killed, Lieutenant Colonel Lubbock was dangerously sick and died in a short time afterwards, so under our "bill of rights" as we believed, we held another election for Colonel and Lieutenant Colonel and to fill some vacancies in line officers where they had resigned and gone home. At this election we chose Captain Wharton of Company B for Colonel, Captain Walker of Company K for Lieutenant Colonel and in Company F, B.E. Joiner Third Lieutenant instead of Wm. Tate, resigned. We continued our scouting, picketing, and patrolling in that section of Kentucky through that severe winter 1861 until February, 1862. In the meantime we received boxes of heavy clothing from our home folks in Texas which was badly needed and duly appreciated, for ours was thread-bare and too light for the

---

[5] Colonel Willich reported the loss of 11 officers and men killed, 22 wounded, 5 missing; Brigadier General Hindman, commanding the Confederates, reported 4 killed and 10 wounded. See *Official Records*, Series I, Vol. VII, pp. 16-20.

cold weather.

Some time in January, I think, Confederate General Zolicoffer [sic] was killed at Fishing Creek and his army defeated, and in February, Fort Donelson on Cumberland River, after two days fighting surrendered to General Grant. These heavy losses caused General Johnston to give up Kentucky and move into Tennessee and select later the Memphis and Charleston railroad as a base of operations.

When the army reached Nashville, our regiment was sent down the river to, or near to, Fort Donelson to gather up some teams and army supplies that had been rushed out there before the surrender of the Fort, while the main body of the Confederates assembled at Murfreesboro, where we rejoined them after bringing those things we had been sent for. After a few days General Johnston moved his infantry and artillery southward to reach his new selected base at Corinth, Mississippi, leaving the cavalry at Murfreesboro to watch the enemies' movements and to impede as much as we might their progress south if an attempt was made to follow in pursuit. In a few days only our regiment and a few squads of other cavalry were to be seen about the city. Among the odds and ends of cavalry men was Captain John H. Morgan, afterwards General Morgan, with a few recruits trying to raise a cavalry command for the Confederate service, and at the same time paying most assiduous attentions to Miss Ready, daughter of Colonel Ready of Murfreesboro.

One night Captain Morgan asked Colonel Wharton for a detail of two men to go with him next day on a raid within the enemy's lines up toward Nashville, telling Colonel Wharton he already had seven men armed and well mounted, and he wished him to furnish him two more good men well mounted with blue overcoats, shotguns and pistols, which would make ten by counting himself. Colonel Wharton sent the order to Company F to make the detail wanted. Jake

Flewellen and I were ordered to report to Captain Morgan
next morning at sun-up, mounted and ready for the trip.
Sunrise came; Captain Morgan and nine private soldiers
moved out on the Nashville pike, mounted and equipped for
the trip according to instructions, except I had on a black
overcoat. I had no blue one and didn't want one and never
did wear one. Morgan assigned me to the rear, thinking and
judging correctly too that the squad would be judged by
those in front and not by one man in the rear. The enemy
had moved their army out on Murfreesboro pike, ten or
fifteen miles, and gone into winter quarters, and were making preparations for a movement south when spring should
come. We kept the turnpike road for several miles and as we
approached the neighborhood of their encampments we
turned to the right and moved through fields and woodland,
sometimes, in full view of their encampments and I thought
uncomfortably near them. But the blue coats of the squad
kept down any suspicion as to our identity and we kept our
course until we were something like five miles from the city
when we approached the pike again, where a thicket of
undergrowth was near to the pike. We stood parallel to the
highway in a line of battle for a short time, when a wagon
train from Nashville loaded with provisions and supplies for
the army drove up, guarded by a troop of cavalry, about
sixteen I think. Armed with sabres, with guns and pistols
pointed at them and a fence between us, they surrendered
readily and the guard and teams and drivers all fell into our
hands without firing a gun. As soon as the wagons could be
fired and the teams and guards could be collected for the
march, Captain Morgan ordered me and three or four others,
including my fellow soldier Flewellen to take charge of them
and get out of the enemy's lines as quickly as possible and
not to halt for anything until we crossed Stone River, near
Murfreesboro, where we should encamp and wait his return.
Our trip being without incident we reached our camping

place about sundown. On the eastern bank of the stream was a large commodious dwelling with a small family in it and servants in the kitchen or cabins and plenty of provender in the barn. We put our prisoners in one of the large rooms and a guard over them and a vidette on or near the river bank; had the servants to feed all the horses at the barn and by alternating in guard and picket duty passed a quiet night.

Next morning before sunrise the vidette reported ten or twelve men advancing towards us from the other side of the river. We supposed them to be Yankees, as the enemy was generally termed by us, but as they drew nearer there were no guns in sight and we decided with much relief that it was Captain Morgan and his men with ten prisoners of war they had captured and kept in the woods all night awaiting daylight so they could see their way to travel better. Captain Morgan, when he reached us related the events of the previous day after we had left him. He said they captured about sixty prisoners and had ordered four men to take them and follow us to Stone River and camp as he had ordered us, and that the enemy's cavalry which had gotten wind of his presence in their lines were looking for him, coming upon this second lot of prisoners, recaptured them and slew three of his men after they had surrendered, one of them making his escape. He further told us that he and his companion had visited a picket post and he, pretending to be officer of the day whose duty required him to look after the guards and pickets of the army, had called to the commander of the post to come out of a house in which he was quartered and as he approached him Morgan placed a pistol to his breast and told him he was his prisoner and for him to make no sign or outcry to his fellows in the house on penalty of death, but to call them out by name, one by one, until all were captured without realizing what had happened. Then his companion was sent out to the picket post a short distance away and brought in the two videttes who were on vidette post, and being late in the evening, the enemy scouting on all sides looking for them, they hid themselves, sat up all night guarding their prisoners and very early in the morning had traveled on until they reached us and now without further delay everything was made ready for the further march into Murfreesboro, that about one mile distant.

We marched up the street in front of Colonel Ready's house, lined up prisoners, horses and spoils and guards across the street while Captain Morgan went in the house and invited his sweetheart and the balance of the family at home to come out on the veranda and see the fruit of his exploit. Flewellen and I were then relieved with thanks and we returned to our company, leaving the prisoners and spoils in the hands of Morgan and his three men he still had with him. Next day one of Morgan's men hunted me up and told me Captain Morgan wanted to see me at his office, so I went with him to the office. The captain greeted me most cordially and said he wanted to thank me over again for the valuable service I had rendered during the scout the day or two before. I told him I did the best I could with the matter I had in hand and did not deserve any special thanks more than others with me. But he seemed to look at the matter differently and said he wished to give me something to be kept as a souvenir of that hazardous venture. He then told me to select a sabre, the best of the captured lot he had and take it with me as a keepsake of the occasion. I did so and took the newest and brightest in the lot and went back to my company with it, and while we served in the same army I don't think now I ever saw him again.

Morgan was captain then, but soon his efficiency as a cavalry officer and raider was conceded on all sides and his promotion was rapid. He made many raids into the enemy's lines, even going one time into Ohio. Men flocked to his standard from Tennessee, Kentucky, Missouri, and other sections. He became Brigadier and later Major-General, I think. He married Miss Ready; was finally killed in Greenville, East Tennessee, in one of his raids in that section. While I prized my sabre as a souvenir, I soon found it was an inconvenience to carry with my other equipments. I had a double barrelled shotgun, two six shooters, my blanket, oil cloth, clothing, haversack, etc., to carry and I could at once see that while it might prove a nice keepsake I had no other use for it. Later on I had a chance to leave it with a relative in middle Tennessee to be kept for me until the war was over or until I should call for it, and in this way it passed the war period; after the close of hostilities I went to see my kinsman (who had died in the meantime) and recovered my sabre from his family who had taken good care of it. It now hangs in the hall of my daughter's home in Grand Rapids, Michigan, 563 Union Ave., S.E. It is her keepsake now, to be disposed of by her as she may desire.

Some time in March, 1862, we, the cavalry forces at Murfreesboro, broke camp and started to follow the army of Tennessee to Corinth, Mississippi, where it was being prepared to act on the defensive against the oncoming armies of General Grant and General Buell. Grant's army was at Pittsburg Landing and encamped out some distance from the landing on the Tennessee River in the direction of Corinth, near Shiloh church, while General Buell was moving his army from Nashville to the same point by forced marches to unite with Grant in his attack on General Johnston, now at Corinth, about fifteen miles south of Pittsburg Landing. Johnston's army consisted of about 40,000 or 45,000 men—my recollection Grant's nearly the same—and Buell's probably 50,000. Johnston decided to attack Grant's army before Buell could reach him and taking one at a time, defeat them both, and I have no doubt his plan would have succeeded had General Johnston lived a few days more. After hastily collecting his forces he moved out of Corinth, on the evening of the fifth[6] of April and next morning before light attacked the enemy in the encampments. The attack was unexpected and furious from the beginning. The enemy was driven slowly back towards the river all day long, making a most stubborn resistance, but gradually they gave up their encampments and artillery and equipments until four o'clock that afternoon when the Confederates were unwisely halted by an order from General Beauregard who succeeded to chief command after General Johnston's fatal wound about three o'clock that afternoon. This closed the first day's engagement with the whole battlefield, including many arms, wagons, sutlers stores, etc., etc., in the hands of the Confederates.

We slept on the battleground that night as best we could with torrents of rain pouring down on us all night and with the gunboats on the river firing over us all night to disturb our slumbers. Many of the boys visited the sutlers stores that night and helped themselves to the edibles and as much clothing as they could use or carry off. Next morning early the Federals having been reinforced by Buell's army, made an attack on us by moving forward against our left, with what was said to be eleven lines of battle, and beat our left wing back some distance and then a movement along all of our front beat back all of our line slowly but surely all day long until night closed the fight with Federals in charge of all their encampments given up the previous day. Thus ended two days of the most terrible fighting I every witnessed before or since. Never did I at any other time hear minie balls seem to fill the air so completely as on this second day's fight. But the battle was not ended yet, for on the third day, the eighth of April, in the evening was an engagement between the

---

[6] Johnston's army left Corinth on the morning of April 3 and arrived in the vicinity of Shiloh late in the afternoon of the 5th.

Confederate cavalry and Federal infantry that ought always to be mentioned as the last act of this tragic event where losses on both sides amounted to more than 20,000 men.[7]

I will now recur to the regiment and company to which I belonged, in order to record their part in this bloody contest and to give some of the incidents of more or less interest that occurred at that time.[8] When the battle commenced on the 6th of April our bugler sounded the assembly which brought us quickly into line. The several companies were numbered to ascertain our effective force at the beginning. Company F numbered 65 men in line, including non-commissioned officers, a captain and second lieutenant. This lieutenant had been elected by the company principally because he had slain two different men in personal combat, and was therefore regarded as a hero of heroes. While the company was being numbered, the musketry one-half mile away was heavy and almost continuous and this officer riding up and down in front of the company remarked time and time again, "Ah, boys, that is music to my ears," making us believe he would perform many deeds of valor when he reached the firing line. At last an order came for us to march to the front and when near there we were ordered to form columns of fours, move to rear of the enemy and make an attack from that quarter; but failing to get far enough back to take them in the rear we marched the head of the column right into the flank of the enemy's line, who, concealed from our view, were lying down behind some timber recently felled by a storm. Being at right angles with our line of march, they could concentrate the fire of their whole line to enfilade our column

---

[7] The losses as officially reported were: Confederates, 10,699; Unionists, 13,047.

[8] Colonel Wharton's report of the battle is to be found in *Official Records*, Series I, Vol. X, Part I, p. 626.

from end to end; and as the head of the column neared them they rose suddenly, poured a volley into us which reached every company in the line of march, killing and wounding men and horses clear back to the rear of column. Of course nothing could be done but fall back and reform for further action in a different move; but I must stop to tell you about this officer to whose ears the battle at a distance was so musical. Though not touched by bullets he became suddenly sick at the sight of bloodshed and had to be sent to the rear to avoid a nervous collapse. It was his first and his last experience in battle for he resigned and returned to Texas and we never saw him again. This lesson is that "the true test of valor comes, not in use of words, but only in action in the crucible of battle."

The regiment was dismounted and made an attack on the enemy on the left flank of our army and then moved to the rear of our army for a support to other troops in firing line, and so fighting and maneuvering was kept up until four o'clock in the afternoon when all the reserves were ordered to the firing line for a final rush to be made as we all thought to drive the panic-stricken army of General Grant into Tennessee River. We formed the line, and awaited the order to move forward. In the meantime the enemy immediately on our front left their line in some haste and disappeared from view over the crest of the hill near the river. While we waited with much impatience for orders to move there came an order from General Beauregard telling that the battle was ended for the day and we had captured General Prentiss with four thousand of his men and a great victory was ours. When the order was read instead of creating enthusiasm amongst the men it created indignation and disgust because it was apparent to all in the firing line that the hard earned victory that had cost so much blood and so many lives was to be thrown away for the want of one more charge which as we thought then and think now would have resulted in a complete overthrow or capture of General Grant's army and the downfall of General Grant himself as a military leader. But why was the Southern army halted at this critical period? General Beauregard's excuse was it was late in the day, the men were tired and needed rest; but the truth as I saw it is the sun was still between three and four hours high and the men were anxious for this last charge to the river, which was not more than one-half mile away, I think. The men talked among themselves of the importance of the movement and their willingness to make it at the time and after events prove but too well the men were right and the commander wrong in issuing the order to halt.

I want to make a little digression from the main story to pay my respects to some erroneous history in regard to this crisis in that battle. Nelson's *Encyclopedia* and the *History of the Mississippi Valley* by Prof. Johnson,[9] Ph.D. and LL.D. of the Agricultural College of Minnesota, I think, both agree substantially in the statement that a hastily constructed battery on the hill near the river and the firing of the gunboats from the river stopped the Confederate's advance. While I am still upon the earth I want to testify as eye-witness at close range, that the aforesaid battery and the gunboat's shelling had no more to do with stopping the forward movement that day than the flowing of the ocean tides or the changes of the moon had to do with it, for nearly an hour had passed since we halted before the battery was placed and before the gunboats fired the first shot and the men had scattered from their commands looking for something to eat. So I enter my protest here and now against the careless and unauthorized way these two authors record history.

---

[9] Possibly Mr. Blackburn has in mind Rossiter Johnson's *History of the War of Secession*, or his *Fight for the Republic*, in each of which a statement of the kind alluded to is made. The name he gives is evidently incorrect.

But to return to my story. There was a man, Charles Howard by name, strong physically and mentally, brave as Julius Caesar and well educated, but with the ways and manners of a frontiersman, with many peculiarities. He had belonged to Company F but got a transfer to Company C for some reason I don't recall. He had gotten a nice laundered white shirt from the sutler's store the night of the 6th of April. Next morning, the 7th, as the regiment was formed to move, some one reproved Howard for tucking his shirt back at the neck, exposing his breast which was one of his habits, telling him it was a shame to treat a nice shirt in that way. His reply was, "If I get shot in the breast today I don't want the bullet to injure my biled shirt." Pretty soon we were ordered to move out towards the enemy and ascertain their position, their probable number, etc., and report back to the commanding general. Our movement, which was only intended for a reconnaissance, drew the fire of the enemy's pickets, for advance in their forward movement had already begun, and one ball struck Howard in the breast a little below the collar bone, going through him and lodging in the muscles or shoulder blade in the back part of his shoulder, not touching his laundered shirt. A little later while we stood in column still headed towards the enemy Howard came riding along the column singing "Blue-eyed Mary," a favorite song of his. As he neared me I said, "Which way, Charles, with your 'Blue-eyed Mary' this morning?" He replied, "To Texas, don't you see my furlough?" pointing to the wound in his breast. He rode horseback to Corinth that day, about fifteen miles, applied for and obtained a furlough soon after, went to Texas and about five months later reported back to his company for duty again, sound as a dollar.

Our next move was to the rear a short distance to dismount and join in with a Louisiana brigade of infantry to make a charge on the enemy. Our movement was down a gentle slope to the bottom of a hill. The enemy came down the slope on the other side towards us. The whole face of the earth at that place and time appeared to be blue and their many lines of battle firing over each others head made a storm of lead that no single line of battle could resist and so after a short time the line was so weakened by losses as to compel the retirement of the remainder. But I want to relate an incident of the battle that impressed me as being out of the ordinary. John P. Humphries, a member of Company F, a brave good soldier carried the largest shotgun I ever saw and always loaded it with about 20 buckshot to each barrel. He had a most peculiar laugh, unlike any laugh I ever heard. As we made that charge that morning there was a small oak tree near the bottom of the hill where the line made a stand. It was right in my front so I got behind the tree thinking it might save my hide somewhat. I had scarcely reached it before Humphries came up behind me. He saw the tree was too small for two to stand behind in safety, so he moved a few steps to the left and got behind another tree about the same size. A little while after I heard Humphries laugh and looked towards him to see what had happened. A minie ball had pierced his hat close to his scalp and knocked it from his head. He grabbed it up, pulled it down hard on his head with both hands and laughed his peculiar laugh again. It occurred to me, and I mentally said, "If you can laugh at that, you will laugh at death when he comes." This repulse was the first experienced in the battle of Shiloh. After this the battle raged pretty well all day over lines resisting with great stubbornness; but by night the enemy occupied their foremost encampments, and our army retreated that night carrying all the army supplies with them as far as was possible to do.

Next day, April 8th, the cavalry were employed in patrolling the space now behind the army and as rear guard we protected as best we could the retreat of our army to Corinth from any possible attack that might be made by the enemy's cavalry or any other arm of service that might pursue it. About four o'clock in the afternoon the enemy's infantry in force kept moving up towards us until we realized we would have to check them by some means to keep them from overtaking the rear of our army. A short distance ahead of us Major Harrison, now commanding the regiment, sent me to General Breckenridge's headquarters who was commanding the rear of the retreating army to tell him of the near approach of a large body of the enemy and to ask him for aid or orders. General Breckenridge's reply was, "Give Major Harrison my compliments and tell him to hold the enemy back awhile for I can't move from here yet." I rode back, delivered the message, and found the enemy had approached to within 250 or 300 yards of our position; had formed two lines of battle and had thrown out skirmishers who were making it lively for our boys who were standing in line on horseback. At this juncture Colonel Forrest came up to us with about an equal number of horsemen to our own, placed them on the right of our line, and being senior officer took charge of the whole line, about two hundred or more in all. He immediately decided to charge so Major Harrison rode up in front of our line, telling us to prepare for the charge, and added, "Boys, go in twenty steps of the Yankees before you turn your shotguns loose on them."

Forrest ordered forward. Without waiting to be formal in the matter, the Texans went like a cyclone, not waiting for Forrest to give his other orders to trot, gallop, charge, as he had drilled his men. By the time the Yankee skirmishers could run to their places in ranks and both lines got their bayonets ready to lift us fellows off our horses, we were halted in twenty steps of their two lines of savage bayonets, their front line kneeling with butts of guns on the ground, the bayonets steading out at right angle or straighter and the rear lines with their bayonets extended between the heads of the men of the first line. In a twinkling of an eye almost, both barrels of every shotgun in our line loaded with fifteen to twenty buckshot in each barrel was turned into that blue line and lo! what destruction and confusion followed. It reminded me then of a large covey of quail bunched on the ground, shot into with a load of bird shot: their squirming and fluttering around on the ground would fairly represent that scene in that blue line of soldiers on that occasion. Every man nearly who was not hurt or killed broke to the rear, most of them leaving their guns where the line went down, and made a fine record in getting back to their reserved force several hundred yards in their rear. After the shotguns were fired, the guns were slung on the horns of our saddles and with our six shooters in hand we pursued those fleeing, either capturing or killing until they reached their reserved force. Just before they reached this force, we quietly withdrew; every man seemed to act upon his own judgment for I heard no orders. But we were all generals and colonels enough to know that when the fleeing enemy should uncover us so their line could fire on us, we would have been swept from the face of the earth.

Some observations might be appropriately made at this time concerning the engagement.[10] It was the last fight of the battle of Shiloh. The enemy turned back from there and we had that section to ourselves. Forrest and his command never fired a gun in that battle for the reason that his military maneuvers as then practiced did not allow his men to get there until the fight was over. Notwithstanding this fact a Memphis paper a day or two afterwards gave out the statement that Colonel Forrest with a few Texans on April the 8th had charged the enemy in force and completely vanquished them. After Forrest gave the order to forward we never saw

---

[10] The official report by Major Harrison is in *Official Records*, Series I, Vol. X, Part I, p. 923.

him any more until we were brigaded over at Chattanooga and put under him for service. We were told that when we made that cyclone movement towards the enemy Colonel Forrest turned to his men to urge them forward faster and was struck in the back by one of the enemy's bullets fired at us as we went at them and had to be taken off the field.[11]

I have been asked by some persons inexperienced as to warfare why the Yankees did not shoot us all off our horses when halted so close in their front. Of course they had no loads in guns to shoot us with and we knew it for as we approached them both lines of battle had fired at us and they had had no time to reload.

There was only one Texan wounded in that fight, Lieutenant Story of Company C, and there is a good reason for that; for the enemy fired when we were crossing a low place in the ground about fifteen yards away and most of their balls went over our heads. One of them struck and mortally wounded Lieutenant Story and one ball took a fur cap off my head leaving, as my comrades afterwards told me, a small powder marked line across my left temple. One or two more incidents of this battle and I will pass on.

In our pursuit of the flying enemy, as I rushed by a stump of a tree, ten feet high and two feet in diameter, looking at a Yankee running in my front a little distance I became suddenly aware of a bayonet near my body in the hands of a red faced Dutchman, and I could not tell whether he made a thrust at me and missed me or whether he intended to use it on me if I bothered him. I turned upon him, fully intending to kill him, but when I leveled my pistol at him, he dropped his bayonetted gun upon the ground and with the greatest

---

[11] For a somewhat different version, see Wyeth, J.A., *Life of N.B. Forrest*, 78-81, or Jordan, Thos., *Campaigns of Forrest and Forrest's Cavalry*, 146-148.

terror depicted in his face, said, "I surrender." In an instant
I forgave him and let him live. I think surrender was the only
English word he could speak, neither could he understand
a word I said. I said, "Take that gun up and break it against
the stump" and when I found he didn't know what to do and
stood trembling I pointed to the gun and made signs to take
hold of it and motions to strike. I got him to understand me,
he broke the breech off and I motioned him to our rear and
he went off at a lively gait.

I had a messmate by the name of Ed Kaylor, a good
soldier, never showing any fear about him. In this battle he
came upon a captain who had vainly tried to rally his men
as they ran to the rear. When he found he could not get them
to stop and help him he concluded he would sell out as best
he could so he fired on Kaylor as he rode towards him. They
exchanged three shots each; Kaylor slowly advancing upon
him. When Kaylor closed in upon him he threw up his hands
and offered to surrender, but Kaylor, in language not suitable
for parlor topics of conversation said, "Oh H—ll you are too
late" and fired another shot, killing him instantly. An eye-
witness to this pistol duel said Kaylor had a broad smile on
his face during this gun play. When I heard of the incident
I said to Kaylor, "Ed, what did you see in that game that
caused you to smile so sweetly at that Yankee?" He said he
was not conscious of having smiled, but he surely did enjoy
that scrap immensely. Poor Kaylor afterwards was killed in
East Tennessee while serving under Longstreet, during the
siege of Knoxville, as related by a Texan companion with him
at the time, as follows: Kaylor and a companion having lost
their horses (in battle or otherwise) were ordered to mount
themselves again by taking horses wherever they could find
them back in the mountains, for the most part of that section
was disloyal to the Confederacy anyway. As they searched
the mountain section for horses they heard that there was
to be a dance given to the Yankee officers near where was

one of their encampments, so they concluded to attend that dance, and mount themselves while the Yankees danced. But after reaching the place they concluded to go in the house, get the riders and take them and their horses both back with them, so they entered the room during the dancing with pistols in hands and demanded surrender of all the men who were in the room, all armed with pistols belted around them. For a time all seemed to go as they wished until some one cried out, "There are only two of these rebels." Then ensued a scuffle for their pistols already in Kaylor's hands and Kaylor began to shoot and several fell from his unerring aim, until some one regained his pistol, shot him and he fell dead among several he had already slain. His companion escaped and lived to tell of his taking off as here related.

But to return to the main story, the Battle of Shiloh was finished. The losses were enormous as already related. Of the sixty-five men and two officers that answered roll call on the morning of the 6th of April of Company F, only fourteen men and the captain answered roll call on the morning of the 8th of April and I was acting orderly sergeant. Now this should not be construed to mean that the other fifty men had been killed or wounded, but it does mean that those not killed or wounded were absent from roll call, most of them off on some kind of duty, such as picketing, scouting, helping the retreating army in whatever way duty assigned them.

The Confederate army collected at Corinth, and the Federal army at Pittsburg Landing, each army where it had encamped before the battle, and each one to plan its future operations was left unmolested for a time. Our regiment was ordered back to Tennessee going through lower middle Tennessee on to Chattanooga. We camped one or two nights at Rienzi, Mississippi, on our way. Awaiting final instructions as to our future movements, news came to us that General Price had reached Corinth with his army of Missourians and Texans. As I had a brother with this command in Whitfield's Legion of Texans I decided to make him a visit before we left Mississippi. It was about twenty miles I think back to Corinth, so getting some papers fixed up by my comrades as a pass to keep me from being arrested as a deserter, I went back to Corinth as my command went eastward on their journey towards Tennessee. My papers were not genuine.

I found my brother sick from exposure during the winter campaign under Price in Missouri. I stayed with him all night and next morning moved out early to overtake my command which was by this time twenty miles and two days journey ahead of me. I rode all day and a part of the night to overtake them. They had captured a small scouting party of Yankees the night or day before I reached them.

Next morning a detail was called for from Company F to take the prisoners back to Corinth, and I was called on to be one of the guards; so back to Corinth I journeyed again, and after delivering the prisoners to General Beauregard's headquarters the following night, and resting a few hours, set out to overtake the command which was moving eastward. After about two days more I was again with the command. But now my faithful steed which I had ridden constantly since the middle of December the year before gave out entirely, worn out by constant usage and had to be left on the wayside, and I had to join the wagon train and to be snubbed as a "wagon dog" by my comrades, a common appellation given to every one who went with the wagons, regardless of the conditions making it necessary for him to be there.

The command went through middle Tennessee and had a fight or heavy skirmish with the Yankees at Sulphur Trestle in Giles County. I do not recall any results of that fight as reported to us except Captain Harris of Company I lost his life there. Arriving at Chattanooga a brigade was organized by putting Forrest's regiment, our regiment, and two Georgia regiments, three or four, I think, together, and Colonel

Forrest took charge of it for service in middle Tennessee and wherever we might be needed.

At that time elections were held in different companies to select commissioned officers where there were vacancies caused by resignations or otherwise. Company F elected two lieutenants, 1st and 2nd, J.K.P. Blackburn 1st, and A.J. Murray 2nd. While we were entitled to commissions issued by the Secretary of War, we never applied for them and never received them. In fact, I don't remember of ever having seen a commission from the government for any officer in the command. The men of the different companies knew whom they had selected and, whether they held commissions or whether they wore insignia of office or not, they always felt that they must obey the men they had elected over them. Hardly a star or bar was to be seen in the command, except in dress parade when the Colonel might show his rank on a dress coat that he kept for the purpose.

Our next encounter with the enemy was in Warren County, Tennessee, near Morrison's depot where the enemy had constructed a stockade and left about three companies of infantry to protect a railroad bridge across the river from destruction by the Confederates. The stockade was built of logs twelve or fifteen inches in diameter and twelve feet long, set on end in trenches two feet deep, close touching each other with portholes cut between the logs about as high as a man's head, to shoot through. These logs were thoroughly tamped in place and a small door left in one side for passing in and out with a screen of like make just on the inside so one going in would pass in the door and turn to left or right to get inside of the stockade. I have been thus particular in describing this fort or stockade so the reader may more easily understand why we were so easily and completely defeated by this small contingent of defenders when we attacked that fort. When within one-quarter or one-half mile of the place Colonel Forrest formed the brigade into single line, ordered

124

us to dismount and then rode in front of each regiment giving instructions about the charge he intended to make. When in front of our regiment he said, "I don't want but one-half of this command for this engagement"—that his scouts reported that only three or four companies were up there and that they had their dinner already cooked, and he wanted us to kill them and then eat their dinner. Company F had thirty men in line, so the first fifteen were ordered to step two paces to the front, and the captain told me to take charge of them, so we maneuvered for some time to get a suitable place to charge from, but could not get nearer than two hundred or two hundred and fifty yards without being exposed to full view of the enemy from the start to the finish, so we were ordered to charge at least two hundred yards through an open field upon that fort. Of course the enemy were inside and had nothing to do but shoot us down from the start. After approaching near enough for some of our men to make telling shots at those portholes we were driven back in much disorder to the timber, back of the field from whence we started. Our loss was estimated at 180 killed and wounded. Company F's loss was one killed and five wounded. The enemy's loss was 20 killed whom we shot in the head through those portholes. James Petty of my company was killed within ten feet of the door of that stockade. These details of the enemy's dead and the place where Petty fell we have learned from our surgeon who was left to care for the wounded at that place.

Our next move was to capture about 2000 soldiers commanded by General Crittenden at Murfreesboro, Tennessee. We started from the neighborhood of McMinnville, Tennessee, one evening in the summer—I don't remember the date[12]—rode until about eight o'clock, stopped, watered

[12] July 12, 1862. The fight was on Sunday, July 13.

and fed our horses, mounted again and rode until nearly daylight to reach our destination. Before we reached the town we captured the videttes on the pike upon which we were moving; also captured General Crittenden in his bed at his headquarters, a nice dwelling in the town, and learned from the citizens that the enemy had an encampment of eight hundred or one thousand infantry soldiers in the suburbs of the town, about the same number and artillery out on Stone River a mile away, and a strong guard over about 150 political or citizen prisoners at the court house.

Colonel Forrest divided his command into three divisions, sending one to attack the court house, one to attack the enemy on Stone River, each division led by a few rangers, and the balance of the rangers to attack the encampment in the edge of Tennessee. The first two bodies mentioned did little except to draw the fire of enemy and to warn them to be ready for us in later attacks. The rangers went into the encampment with a yell and attacked the enemy as they came out of the tents in their night clothes and after a lively skirmish in which many of them fell, our Colonel Wharton was wounded and ordered the regiment to withdraw.

Afterwards Colonel Forrest collected all of our regiment behind a block of buildings near the encampment, sent in a flag of truce demanding unconditional surrender of the encampment within thirty minutes and added, "If you refuse I will charge you with the Texas Rangers under the black flag." After a little delay they agreed to surrender and immediately Colonel Forrest sent flags of truce to other places where the troops were with the same demand and same threat and added, "I have your General and all the balance of his command as prisoners in my hands." In a little while the whole of General Crittenden's army were our prisoners with all their artillery, wagons, teams and army and soldiers' supplies and about 2000 soldiers. Forrest had played a bold game of bluff and it had succeeded where we could scarcely hope to conquer by force of arms; for our number was about half, and half of that number were fresh troops who had never been under fire of battle before.

An incident occurred as we made the charge along the streets in the twilight of that morning which was both inspiring and impressive. The ladies in their night robes came out on the pavement and cheered with their shouts and their "God bless you," even when the enemy's bullets were flying about them.

All army stores and artillery, small arms and ammunition were put under guard to take them back to McMinnville, about forty or fifty miles (I cannot remember exactly). The troops were collected and a guard of two companies and a commissioned officer were called for to take charge of them and march them back to McMinnville. Companies F and D of our regiment were detailed for this purpose and I was ordered to take charge of them and see to it that they were delivered to the place of rendezvous. I formed a column of prisoners, eight abreast and closed them up so as to allow only walking room between them, and put some guards in front on horseback, some in the rear, and the balance on each side; thus enclosing prisoners in hollow square and gave command to move forward. I gave instructions to the guards so the prisoners could hear, "If any man makes a break from that column, shoot him down without halting him." This was near sundown and we moved without difficulty but slowly on account of the long distance the prisoners had to walk; rushing them would have resulted in breaking them down.

My guards had had no sleep now for about forty hours nor rest either, so I soon found they were asleep on their horses, and fearing the enemy might discover it and make their escape I had to use heroic methods to meet the emergency. So I rode around that moving column all night punching or pinching the guards to keep them awake. They would generally respond by "All right" or some sign as I waked them, but as soon as I passed they would fall asleep again so my march around that column continued on and on.

Just before daylight, I received order from Colonel Forrest to park my charge in a grass lot, put out videttes and let them rest an hour or so. So I readily obeyed instructions. By the time that I had placed the guards, the prisoners had all fallen on the ground and were asleep. My guards also fell asleep and I after strenuous efforts to keep up and look after the business in my hands, fell asleep also, my horse remaining by me. When daylight came I was the first to stir. I awaked the guards and then the prisoners, adopted the same formation I had before. We were soon on the march again with still about fifteen miles to travel.

We reached Forrest's headquarters about nine o'clock, turned over the prisoners to him, and asked him for the camp of the regiment. I dismissed the guard, went to camp, and found our captain and a few men with him. I dismounted, leaving my horse with the saddle and personal baggage on him for some one else to look after and fell down on the bare ground and slept until after sundown that evening without having had water or anything to eat for about twenty-four hours. The last I had was from the sutler's store the evening before. When I got up I found my horse dead only a few steps from where I left him. He had died from exhaustion. The two days and two nights constant going on the light feed he got were too much for him and he perished in the service of his country, so to speak.

I can think of nothing of much interest occurring to any portion of our regiment until General Bragg with the army of Tennessee made a raid into Kentucky in September, 1862, I think. The cavalry of course was to be the vanguard on this trip in order to clear up the way, and keep the commanding general posted as to what was before him on his line of march.

Our first engagement was with McCook's corps near the Kentucky-Tennessee line when our regiment was ordered to feel of the enemy in that section to ascertain its strength and size of force. This resulted in several casualties to our men and in finding it was McCook's corps marching north to be ready for General Bragg when he should get there. S.G. Clark of our company was one of the killed here. I kept a diary of the trip through Kentucky on this raid and while I lost it soon after the raid was over I remember some of the entries made. One was that from the day we entered Kentucky until the day we passed out of the state, thirty-eight days, our regiment in part or as a whole had been under the fire of the enemy's guns forty-two times, including Perryville Battle as one of the times. Fighting and skirmishing occurred every day and some days more than once.[13] Except at Perryville our losses were generally light, but coming so frequently they amounted to many in the aggregate.

Before I leave Perryville in my narrative I shall relate incidents on that field not to be easily forgotten. My bedfellow during the trip was D.A. McGenagil. At Perryville, a piece of shell bursting in our line of battle struck him in the side, breaking two of his ribs. He was sent off to the hospital for repairs so I was without a bedfellow that night, and as the nights were frosty I looked out for some other person to get the benefit of his blanket for a covering while mine should be spread on the ground for the pallet. We only had one blanket each, hence the necessity of having a partner. The battle had continued to rage until eight o'clock at night or thereabouts, the Confederates driving back their antago-

---

[13] The report of Gen. Jos. Wheeler of the cavalry operations in Kentucky is found in *Official Records*, Series I, Vol. XVI, part 1, pp. 893-900. Wharton's report is not found.

nists steadily until the firing ceased. Our regiment was required to go on picket along the space where the last fighting was done. It was in a corn field near a little branch. The Federals had withdrawn but a short distance without noise, and without fires had retired after putting out their pickets on the side next to us. We were instructed to go to the place to be picketed with great caution and keep silent. We found the place we stopped on and had to stay that night on ground covered with flint rocks from the size of a man's fist to the size of his head and many dead of both armies lying around. The wounded had been removed, or most of them. I looked around or searched around among my company; we only had a poor star light, as it was mostly cloudy. I found Sam Woodward of my company with a good blanket and no bedfellow for the night, and we soon arranged to bunk together. I said, "Sam, you look for a place as smooth as you can find, as clear of the flint rock as possible, and let me know and we will fix for bed." In fifteen or twenty minutes he came to me said, "I have found a fairly good place, but there are two dead men on it." I said, "They are as dead as they will ever be, are they not?" He said, "Yes," and I said, "Then we will remove them a little space and occupy their place." He said, "All right," and we went to the spot selected and turned one man over one way and the other the other way (they were lying parallel with each other), made our bed between them and slept sweetly until daylight next morning; and behold one of the dead was a Confederate and other one a Federal soldier. Both had fallen on the same spot and died near each other.

Some of our boys, nearly barefooted, were searching around among the dead for footwear, all in the darkness. They had to judge of what they were getting by the way it felt. Mullins of Company D found a good pair of boots on Wheeler, I think, another ranger who was asleep among the dead. He immediately decided the boots would suit, grabbed one of them, and jerked it off Wheeler's foot. This aroused Wheeler to consciousness and he called out, "What in the h-ll are you doing there?" "Nothing, d—n you, I thought you were dead and I needed those boots." John P. Humphries, of whom I have spoken before, needed footwear and went out after daylight to see what were the chances. He found a Yankee, dead, sitting against a tree, with a good pair of shoes. John got down on his knees to take off the fellow's shoes and, just as he got one unlaced and ready to pull off, took another glance at the Yankee's face and the Yankee winked at him. He left the shoes on his dead man and came to camp and told it, and laughing that peculiar laugh, said he didn't want any shoes anyway.

Next morning our army moved to Harrodsburg, Kentucky, and the other army stayed near where they had camped before, not seeming to want to follow us, except at a considerable distance from us.

One other incident of the Perryville Battle I will mention. There were two young men, about eighteen and twenty years old, brothers, named George and Simeon Bruce who came to Texas to live, from Vermont, about eight months before the commencement of hostilities. They had no relatives or interests in Texas, but when the war came up they volunteered in our regiment, saying the South was right in its contentions, and they freely offered their lives in its defense. At Perryville Simeon Bruce was shot through the calf of his leg with a grapeshot and George was left with him to care for him. They communicated with homefolks in Vermont and told of their whereabouts and conditions. An answer soon came back with money for every need and urging their return home. They were informed, also, that one of their brothers was a colonel in the Federal army and another one a surgeon in the same army. The family where they were staying also urged them to go home when they learned the facts concerning them. The boys didn't entirely consent to return, but said

131

they would give it favorable consideration, not fully committing themselves to any certain course, but rather left the impression when Sim recovered they might go home. Sim after a long time got so he could ride horseback without much discomfort and then the boys bought horses with the money sent them and hastened South to their command and remained with it, making splendid soldiers until the war ended and returned to Texas and are there or in Oklahoma yet, or were when I last heard from them. When they returned to us I said, "I love my country and have offered my life in her defense, but I believe you Bruce boys are truer patriots than I am." As to the losses in this battle, I cannot recall. It was quite sanguinary and losses were heavy on both sides.

After the battle of Perryville the Confederate army moved towards Cumberland Gap in eastern Kentucky. The Federal army followed at a safe distance; our cavalry was rearguard to the Confederates. Skirmishes light and heavy with the enemy's advancing column was our daily pastime, sometimes twice or three times a day. Rations became scarcer day by day as we traversed the poor mountainous regions of eastern Kentucky. The people in there were generally poor with small patches in cultivation and few live stock, and all they had to live on had been consumed by the infantry which preceded us; so it must be clear to the reader that the cavalry suffered for want of food supplies. They were kept too busy to make excursions off the line of march to get food so they fasted and fought for days without anything worth mentioning. I saw men trimming beef bones left by the infantry, where they had killed the beeves and issued the meat to the men, thus getting a little of the stringy leaders off of them. Then they would break them and get the marrow inside. I saw a number of men, of whom I was one, pick out the scattered grains of corn tramped in the ground by some infantry officer's horse where he had been fed a day or two ahead of us, and eat them with a relish, thus proving the adage that hunger is a good appetizer.

One day we were fighting a large force of the enemy's infantry and our Colonel thinking we would not be able to check them sent to our infantry for help. A brigade of our men came back to our assistance, and General B.F. Cheatham came with them, but they reached us after we had driven the enemy back and didn't need their help. General Cheatham had eight or ten ears of corn tied on his saddle behind him to feed his horse. A hungry Texan spied him and said, "Old man (addressing Cheatham), I will give you a dollar apiece for those ears of corn." The general with a haughty, dignified look said, "Do you know whom you are talking to?" The soldier said "No, and I don't care a damn, but I will do what I said I would about that corn." The general smiled, untied his corn, and threw it to the hungry men who scuffled over it as very hungry hogs would have done.

In a few more days we passed out of Kentucky through Cumberland Gap, moved on to Knoxville, Tennessee, and camped a few days to rest. The first night we were at Knoxville it snowed all night and next morning the ground and the army was covered with a three inch snow. We had no tents or covering of any kind, but our sleep was sound and restful. The leaves were still green on the trees and the contrast in colors between the leaves and the snow was quite impressive, and very unusual. This was in October, 1862, if my memory serves me correctly.

From Knoxville the army moved to middle Tennessee. Our regiment was camped at Nolensville, about fifteen or twenty miles south of Nashville. Our duty was to watch the movements of the Yankee army now assembling at Nashville and to keep our general posted about them. We remained at this point until Christmas Day. Some of the boys were preparing to have an egg-nog for Christmas when suddenly our pickets were driven in and reported a large force of infantry and artillery moving upon us. The regiment was mounted at once to meet this advance. As soon as we come in full view of the enemy they opened fire with artillery, four guns throwing what seemed to be about six pound shells. I was in command of Company F that day, the captain being on the sick list but still in camp. As we moved in columns of twos in front of the enemy their shells got our range pretty quickly. One shell burst in rear of my company doing slight damage, another one entered the body of a horse near my horse's head, bursting inside the horse and knocked my horse to his knees and covering him and me with blood and flesh from the other horse. Strange to say the trooper riding this torn up horse escaped without the slightest injury. His name was Glasscow of Company C; he was riding in the rear of his company in front of me. A few steps further another shell passed between my horse's head and the rear of another horse ridden by Lieutenant Black, cutting down a cedar tree as large as a man's leg, just on the left of us. We moved further to the left out of range of this artillery, dismounted, formed a line and moved out towards, or to the left of this battery somewhat; but before we made the attack a flanking command was discovered moving to our rear on the right and we returned to our horses and rode over to the right of the first alignment to meet this flank movement and while engaging these with a furious fire another force equally strong was approaching from the front and we had to retire for a new alignment.

Colonel Harrison, passing by me as we had begun to retire before the enemy, said, "Form your company on this rise and hold the position while I form the regiment behind you in supporting distance." I called on my men to fall into line, but they had turned towards the rear and the heavy firing of the enemy from two points made it almost impossible for men or horses to get their consent to face the other way and stand still; so I urged and I ordered with all the vehemence I possessed, sometimes getting as many as two or three to face about and make a temporary halt and then move on. Finally Gabe Beaumont of Company A, who had fallen behind his company in the different movements, seeing my trouble said to me "Lieutenant, I will stand; form your company on me." He took his stand, I rushed my men in line with him, and having got my men in line was riding up and down the line encouraging all I could to stay there. The enemy's bullets were flying uncomfortably thick. I heard a ball strike when near Beaumont and saw his gun fall, but he stood perfectly still until I approached him. I asked Gabe, "Are you badly hurt?" He said, "I think I am." I said, "I will excuse you now. You can retire and my men will stay here without you." So I sent him off with a man to help him if he needed help. This ball shivered his left arm just below the shoulder joint and had to be taken off at the shoulder to save his life. He was shot out of service, but he demonstrated to his comrades in arms what true bravery could accomplish. I met this brave hero many years after in Coleman, Texas. He had studied medicine after the war and made a success in that profession. A while after Beaumont was sent to the rear, the Colonel sent me word to withdraw my company and fall back to my position. This ended the fighting for the day, and that night, after viewing the enemy's encampments with Company F, trying as best I could to make an estimate of their numbers and reporting the same to the Colonel, we rested.

The regiment moved to Murfreesboro where two armies were rapidly gathering for one of the great battles of the Civil War. Just whether we moved that night, or fell back gradually as the enemy advanced to Murfreesboro I cannot now recall, but on the first day of January, 1863, brigade skirmish line was formed from our brigade and I was ordered to take charge of this line. The men were placed in line ten feet apart on foot in one side of an old field grown up in long weeds about as high as a man's head. The enemy were in the other side of the same field. Our skirmishers were armed with rifles or muskets for the occasion. I was told to keep the men to their places so there would be no weak spot and no bunching of our men on the line, to keep them firing continually, etc., etc. As I rode along that long line of men—I was the only man on horseback in that line—I saw that Bill Simpson of Company F was about two feet, or three feet at the most, from a high poplar stump in line with the men, so I said, "Bill, take the stump. There it is but a little ways from your place and it may save your life or your limbs." He looked up at me and said, "I thank you, I am doing very well here," and refused to use it. These two lines of skirmishers were in what was afterward known as the left flank of our army during the battle and as far as I am able to tell now this was the beginning of that great battle.

We were relieved after a while by some infantry and we remounted our horses to meet some Yankee cavalry that came in on our left. We charged them, drove them, and scattered them. As we returned from pursuing them my horse slipped and fell, throwing me on the horn of my saddle and producing a case of nearly strangulated hernia from a slight rupture I had had before. This fall laid me up for several days and took me off the battlefield until the battle ended and longer. Whatever else I relate of this battle or as to what happened in or to the regiment must be from hearsay and not from personal observation. The regiment was engaged all the time, sometimes in the flank, sometimes in the rear of the enemy; sometimes fighting infantry, sometimes cavalry; capturing many of the enemy and destroying much of his supplies.

One or two incidents I wish to relate happened during that conflict. A Yankee General fell into the hands of the Rangers. They asked him his name and rank. He said, "General Willich." "The same who commanded the 32nd

Indiana Infantry as Colonel?" he was asked. "Yes the same, and who are you," demanded the General. "Terry Texas Rangers" was the reply. "Mein Gott," said General Willich, "I had rather be a private in that regiment than to be a Brigadier General in the Federal army." Willich had met the boys at Woodsonville, Ky., as Colonel of the 32nd Indiana regiment and had met them at Murfreesboro as Brigadier General and had lost out both times and was qualified to judge of their military prowess. General Willich was Dutch or German, with a foreign accent.

Colonel Harrison by this time had so long escaped personal injury from shot and shell, his men dubbed him "Old Iron Sides," because as they said he was sheathed with iron and no bullet could penetrate his body. On the second day of this battle, Billy Sayers, his Adjutant, sat on his horse beside him under a heavy fire. Colonel Harrison leaned over to Sayers and whispered, "I am wounded, but don't say anything about it on account of the men." Billy wanted him off the field, but he refused to go. It proved to be a flesh wound in the hip, not very serious, and he stayed with and commanded the regiment throughout the battle. On another occasion the Colonel, while standing in front of his line ready to make or receive a charge as it might happen, was looking through his field glass at a body of cavalry some distance off. Suddenly he exclaimed, "Now boys, we will have some fun. There is a regiment out there preparing to charge us, armed with sabres. Let them come up nearly close enough to strike and then feed them on buckshot." So they came up with great noise and pretense, hoping to demoralize and scatter their opponents and then have a race in which they could use their sabres effectively. But as the Texans stood their ground the Yankees ran up to within a few steps and halted suddenly, giving our boys the chance they were wishing for. One volley from the shotguns into their ranks scattered these sabre men into useless fragments of a force.

Many of them surrendered and our boys quizzed them with merciless questions. "Why did you stop?" "Are your sabres long ranged weapons?" "How far can you kill a man with those things?" After a conflict lasting two days with varying success and defeat for both armies, the Southern army withdrew to the south, leaving the other army with fresh reinforcements encamped not far from the last lines of battle the evening before.

The weather had turned fearfully cold and the earth would freeze very hard at night. About the first night after we left Murfreesboro Jim Stevenson, coming off of duty late, came to the log heap fire of my mess, and asked permission to sleep near our fire. Jim was a shiftless boy whose dress was weather worn and untidy, his body generally dirty and infected with what the boys called "graybacks." So no one would sleep with him and he didn't expect any one to divide bedding with him. We granted his request and he made his pallet down a little space from the rest of us and went to sleep. Next morning he slept on after daylight. I went to see how he was faring and to awake him if still living. I caught his top blanket at his head and raised it up and as it was set and frozen it stood up on the other end like a dried raw hide would do with like handling. I said, "Get up my boy, don't try to sleep all day. How did you sleep?" He replied, "Bully," that he had two blankets last night. He had an old thread bare blanket under him and a heavy army blanket he had captured from the enemy during the battle just fought. He had slept all night without moving, as evidenced by an unfrozen streak, just the shape of his body on that blanket where he had lain on his side; the rest of that blanket being frozen stiff as a board. Jim could suffer hardships without a murmur, and although he was shiftless and loved to play poker he could always be depended upon when there was any fighting to be done. He was a brave man and a good soldier.

The army remained at Shelbyville, Tennessee, for some

time, then moved on south by way of Tullahoma to Chattanooga and encamped there. Our individual regiment acting as scouts and guards for the rear moved leisurely along after our army, delaying the enemy's movements as far as they might attempt to follow.

After we passed Tullahoma, I don't remember seeing another blue coat until the battle of Chickamauga, which took place in the following September, the 19th and 20th. Our line of march was along the Nashville, Chattanooga and St. Louis Railroad until we reached Chattanooga, and then we were allowed to move down to Rome, Georgia, where we had a much needed rest of two weeks which, with a few days at Woodburn, Kentucky, constituted our entire rest up to this time.

It may be well at this time to mention the fact that while up in Kentucky General Forrest was taken from us and returned to Tennessee to raise a new command of cavalry. He took with him his old regiment and from that time up to the battle of Chickamauga our regiment again acted as an independent command.

After our resting spell we were ordered to rejoin the army. Rosecrans with a large force had compelled General Bragg to retire towards Chickamauga a few miles south of Chattanooga. Here the two armies met in one of the bloodiest battles of the Civil War, continuing two days and resulting in a complete victory for the Confederates; but the victory was won at a fearful cost. General Forrest had by this time raised a new command and during this battle he and his men won immortal fame by fighting the enemy on foot and driving them, capturing their artillery and proving to all who were disposed to doubt the effectiveness of cavalry in warfare that they could vie with the infantry in infantry service when called upon. Some one speaking of Forrest's success at Chickamauga said he had glorified the cavalry by showing they could win victories against great odds on foot as well as on horseback.

Our regiment was engaged only twice during the battle and that was when Federal cavalry tried to attack our army from the rear. In one of these attacks we met and defeated the Fourth Ohio Cavalry, mortally wounding their colonel and driving them off, leaving their dead and wounded on the field. We passed back over the field, and the Colonel still living and gasping for breath was sitting with his back against a tree. Some of our boys approached him and said to him, "Well, Colonel, as you will not need your hat or boots any longer, we beg the privilege of exchanging with you," and as the Colonel could not reply, the boys concluded that silence gives consent, and proceeded to make the exchange.

For the balance of the time our duties kept us policing and guarding during that battle rather than fighting. The Federal army returned to Chattanooga and our army took position near there on Missionary Ridge and Lookout Mountain, where other battles occurred later on. Our regiment moved up on the Tennessee river, where we picketed on the river. On the opposite side at the time was the Fourth Ohio Cavalry also on picket duty. The pickets talked to each other across the stream and found out they were somewhat acquainted from personal contact at Chickamauga and some other point which I cannot recall; also feeling there should be no animosity existing between men who had faced each other in battle, they arranged for a truce, a suspension of hostilities until they could have a swim, a few yarns, swap tobacco for coffee, exchange newspapers and have a good time generally. A Yank said to Johnnie Reb,—these were the endearing names we were accustomed to give each other, "Where is Old Ironsides (our Colonel) today?" "At camp," says Johnnie Reb, "Where is Colonel So-and-so?" (calling by name the colonel of the Fourth Ohio) "Oh the devil, you know where we left him over at Chickamauga," was the answer. These truces were common in all parts of the army when it could be arranged without a commissioned officer being present. They could not afford to participate because of position and commission. I believed then, and I still believe now, if the terms of peace had been left to the men who faced each other in battle day after day, they would have stopped the war at once on terms acceptable to both sides (except the civil rulers) and honorable to all alike. These men that always bore the brunt of battle never had and never will have any bad feelings towards each other.

Some time in October news reached us that one hundred wagons, loaded with provisions for Rosecrans army had started from Nashville to Chattanooga to feed his army. Provisions had become very scarce, and the railroad was torn up so they could get nothing over it. Hence it was necessary for them to use wagons to transport their supplies. A brigade of cavalry was organized at once consisting of the 8th Texas, which was our regiment, the 11th Texas, 3rd Arkansas, and 4th Tennessee regiments and placed under command of General Joe Wheeler. General Forrest was ordered to turn over his command to General Wheeler. This order aroused the wrath of Forrest, who contended that he should be in chief command. General Wheeler started on a raid through middle Tennessee to capture and destroy that wagon train and to do the enemy any damage he could otherwise.[14] We met the wagon train in Sequachie Valley, all loaded heavily, with four good mules to each wagon. We burned the train, while the guards with the train deserted it for safety in the mountains close by. We killed most of the mules, amounting to hundreds, only saving a few to take the places of some wornout horses in our commmands and other needs we might have on the trip, such as substitutes for

---

[14] For Wheeler's report of this raid, see *Official Records*, Series I, Vol. XXX, Part II, pp. 722-725.

ambulance work and for artillery service when it became necessary to make such changes. This destruction of the train was a great waste of food and other army supplies, but we felt it was but just punishment for the invaders and destroyers of our country. We moved into middle Tennessee.

By the time we reached Warren County, General Mitchell (author of Mitchell's Geography) had gathered an army of mounted infantry and was in pursuit of us. Once upon the mountains, Colonel Harrison had to form a line of battle and show fight to protect our rear guard who had been run into by the Federals. We stood in line some time for them to come in sight so we could charge them, but instead of coming on they stayed back in some bushes and ran up a battery of their guns and began to shell us pretty heavily. I was in command of Company F and while sitting on my horse in front of my company I noticed most of the shells were coming or seeming to come over my company and the shots were getting lower every time. I looked for a reason and found that four of the men were riding white horses and had accidentally gotten bunched together in the line; this affording a fine target for the enemy's guns, so I ordered one of these men to go quickly and ask permission of Colonel Harrison for me to dismount my men. I had ordered him to go quickly and he galloped or run his horse up to head or right of regiment (my company being in left of same). In less time than it takes to write this my man returned and said "Colonel Harrison says 'No. Keep your men on their horses.'" I called at once, "Attention, Company F; dismount, lie down flat on the ground and hold your bridle reins in your hand." Just as the order was obeyed, a shell struck one of these white horses in the breast, tearing off his shoulder and doubtless would have taken off the leg of the rider if he had been on him. I had thus disobeyed orders, which is always dangerous and is condemned by the authorities on military tactics, but I found consolation in the fact that I had saved the life that would have been uselessly sacrificed, as I looked at it. Soon an order came from General Wheeler for us to fall back. Our loss was only one man killed in Company C, and some horses. This man might have been saved if Company C had been dismounted as was Company F.

The enemy didn't trouble us much more after this until we reached Farmington, in Marshall County, Tennessee. We had passed through Shelbyville the previous day and as Northern merchants had come into that town with an abundance of all kinds of merchandise, groceries, including liquors, wares, etc., our men considered that those goods were contraband, since they belonged to army followers, and they helped themselves liberally to such things as they thought they needed; the officers only forbidding the taking of whiskey. But most of the soldiers managed to get some in their canteens to take with them for future emergencies; so the next day the rear guard, imbibing too freely, got on a spree and while they were having the time of their lives the Federal mounted infantry ran into them, captured and scattered the whole guard and closed upon the moving column of General Wheeler's army, so that he had to give battle at Farmington to protect himself. General Wheeler unlimbered his artillery near the pike and commenced a rapid fire. The enemy replied in kind with several guns. While this artillery firing was going on a courier was sent for us who were four or five miles north of Farmington near Duck river. The order was to come to Farmington double quick, which meant a gallop all the way. The enemy had moved a regiment in a column of two or double ranks close order up to within 250 yards of General Wheeler's battery and parallel to the pike and they were armed with Spencer rifles as we learned later on. This movement was being made on foot, notwithstanding they were mounted men. Their horses had been left in the rear. Company F was in front that day at the head of the column of regiment and I was commanding the company. As we approached General Wheeler, he gave an order to our Colonel who was riding by my side to "form fours, move up the pike until you draw fire of the enemy, then charge them."

There was a drizzle of rain, the smoke from the artillery was lowering, and the enemy were obscured from our view until we were probably 75 yards from them. The enemy on our approach had formed along parallel the pike on the west side of it and fired a volley from their whole line into our columns of four, aiming at the sound of our horses' feet, for we were still obscured from their view by the smoke, but that volley found victims all the way down the regiment, striking every horse excepting one at the head of the column and about a dozen men in Company F. When that volley was fired Colonel Harrison ordered me to lead the charge; and with a yell, answered by many still unhurt along the column, I shouted as loud as I could, "Charge them, Rangers!" Colonel Harrison dropped out to one side and as the other companies came rushing on he would say to them, "Follow Blackburn." The yell and the rattle and roar of horses feet on the pike was too much for the enemy's nerves and they broke back up the pike. A high cedar rail fence along the pike on the side they were on kept them from scattering out far that way, and so they ran back like frightened sheep until they seemed to be twenty or more deep when we reached them and still pressing back away from us. When I had gone along the side of this fleeing mass as far as any one seemed to be following me, I turned into the fleeing column with my six-shooter with all of the energy and expedition I could.

As I passed a small elm tree not more than four inches in diameter I think, where a few men, four or five, had stopped for protection, one of them put his gun within a few inches of my left thigh and fired. I saw the gun just as it fired, but not in time to knock it down. The bullet passed through both of my thighs, cutting a branch artery and fracturing the bone in my right limb, and as the bone did not break the ball glanced and came out on top of my leg. The blood from the artery followed, spurting for a short time. I had fired three or four shots up this time at close range that enabled me to reach the men crowding against me, but when I saw the flow of blood following that wound I had no inclination to continue the performance, so I turned my horse to ride to the rear. As I turned I found my Sergeant, Ledbetter, at my side engaged in the same game I was leaving, but before my horse could get a start the Sergeant's horse was killed and fell suddenly, falling against my horse, nearly knocking him down with his fall. I saw Ledbetter was fastened under his horse, his foot having been caught under him. I rode to the rear.

Just at this juncture another enemy regiment came up on the right side and fired a volley into our regiment, which began to retire slowly and in order. I rode on through the village and on to a little creek nearby, where I found four or five of my men whose horses had been killed by the first volley of the enemy as we had charged. They had retired there for safety after being dismounted so unceremoniously. When I reached them my horse began to stagger and seeing he was going to fall I asked my men to take me off of him and by the time they had placed me on a blanket on the ground my steed fell dead with six bullets in his body, any one of which would have proven fatal, so my men reported. Noble steed, he had been with me in many battles, but this was his last one and I will say it was also my last battle, for I was a prisoner of war on parole of honor for the balance of the time.

The battle of Farmington was now over and the enemy held the field, but attempted no pursuit. Other Confederate commands had been fighting there before we came into the fray, but had yielded to the onslaught of superior numbers. I do not know the losses on either side, but I saw an account of the battle of Farmington a few days afterwards in a

145

Northern paper which reported Wheeler's losses at 300 killed and wounded and Mitchell's losses at 180 killed and wounded. I know that was an exaggerated report so far as our losses were concerned and rather think it was concerning Mitchell's losses.

A just criticism of the regiment of soldiers we charged that day might be penned here. Situated and formed as they were so that their entire fire could be concentrated on the pike, and armed as they were with repeating rifles, they missed an opportunity that rarely comes to a command in warfare to annihilate a whole regiment of their antagonists by standing their ground and firing their guns already loaded in hand; for fourteen volleys well aimed as the first one would have destroyed our command without a loss of one of their own men. But their cowardly feet took them away and lost to them this opportunity.

Three or four men left on the field were taken in by the citizens close by, of whom I now call to mind, Steve and Dick Jarmon, and George Chandler. Ledbetter made his escape from under his horse in a miraculous manner. He said afterwards that he tried his best to pull his foot from under the horse, but as he had a new cavalry boot on that foot and that tied with a stout leather string above his knee as was the custom he decided that it couldn't be done; so he continued to shoot at this new command approaching from the east side of turnpike with his pistol, thinking he could surrender to them after his pistol was emptied. As the enemy drew nearer they discovered he was a red headed man and ordered him in a most indecent way to surrender "a red headed ———." They continued to fire at him, seeing he was not obeying their orders, when one of their balls struck him between the second and third fingers of his left hand, going through his hand and arm up to the elbow and coming out there. He said the pain seemed to give him the strength of a giant and with another trial he brought out his foot, leaving his boot under the dead horse. He rose and broke to run. W.H. Harris, another member of Company F as he slowly retired to the rear, turned his horse, and galloped back and met him. Ledbetter sprang on the horse behind Harris and rode away in a gallop out of danger. In the meantime the enemy beholding the daring feat quit firing and cheered Harris for his brave act which saved a wounded comrade.

After my horse's death I turned over my pistols, saddle, bridle, blanket, etc., and another horse I had back with the baggage wagon to Sam Street one of Company F and asked him to take care of them for me. I was placed on a blanket and carried by four comrades to the rear to get beyond reach of the bullets which were still falling around us from the enemy's guns. As we moved along bunched up that way the enemy would fire at us, for we made a good target for them. I could hear the balls striking the ground around us and begged my men to leave me there and save themselves. They refused and said if I could stand it they could, and took me on and out of reach of the enemy's fire (for they did not follow us up) and found an ambulance, put me in that and carried me on about six miles further to Lewisburg, Tennessee. Here they left me in the house of Mr. McKnight, who with his wife lived alone, both of them well advanced in years, but both as good and kind as possible for most people to be. Our surgeon had made only a casual examination of me, had given me a dose of morphine and a glass of brandy when I was first taken off my horse, and then went on to the other wounded, without seeming to realize I was bleeding so profusely as to endanger my life. But when we reached Lewisburg, I was so exhausted from loss of blood that Dr. McClure, a local physician there who looked at me, told my attendants it was necessary to leave me there if they expected to save my life. So I was left there so weakened that I could not raise my head from my pillow.

That night Wheeler's command moved on southward five

or six miles and camped. Next day about nine o'clock General Mitchell's army came into Lewisburg and halted there for some hours and while there his surgeon busied himself looking up the wounded who had been able to get that far from the battlefield, of whom there were several. When he came in to see me he examined me pretty closely and said "This right thigh has a fracture and must be taken off at the hip joint." I uttered my protest with all the strength I could command and said, "No, it will not be taken off." He replied, "It will kill you if left on." I said, "Let it kill me." He replied, "If you are fool enough to risk it, it is all right with me." I said, "I am fool enough to risk it, for when that leg goes to the grave I am going with it." He asked my rank, I think, and left.

Pretty soon Mitchell's Adjutant General came in. He said he came over to parole me by Mitchell's order. I said, "Read me the terms and conditions of parole." He read, "Pledge your honor never to fight any more against the United States forces until you are duly exchanged. You report to the nearest United States forces as soon as you are able to walk. Will you sign it and keep it?" he asked. I said, "I will," so he handed me the paper and pen and I signed, lying flat on my back. Of all the wounded left there at Farmington I was the only one paroled that I heard of.

My men left at Farmington were kindly cared for by the citizens and were constantly watched and movements reported to Federal authorities by Union men who were to be found in many sections, now that the Union forces had possession of the State. These Union men sympathized generally with the Yankees, and wished them success. Before these men of Company F were supposed to be able to travel they escaped south by the aid of some secret scouts who were operating in the State in behalf of Southern leaders. Steve Jarmon the worst wounded one was put on a lounge or pallet on a mule's back and tied on and transported in that way south to his company, while the others rode horseback by his side to their destination. Steve recovered sufficiently for light service and remained to the end, but never got well and died from the effects of his wound many years after the war closed, so his wife afterwards told me. I recall a few names of the killed and wounded outside of my company in the battle of Farmington. John Martin Lane of Company A was killed. He had a sister living in Pulaski, Tennessee, who came for the body and buried it at Brick Church, the former burying ground of his family. A.G. Love of Company C, I think, was killed and buried there. Some of his kinsfolk living at Culleoka came for his body, exhumed it, and buried it at Culleoka, Tennessee. Lieutenant Hunter was killed there and buried there. I think he belonged to Company H. Major A.P. Christian was shot in the mouth and several jaw teeth knocked out, and the bullet came out under his right ear. Jones, of Company A, was shot in the head, but not fatally wounded. About fourteen soldiers killed there were buried in one grave by the citizens of the neighborhood, and they erected a monument over them, or for them since the war. This battle was fought on October 7, 1863.

Dr. R.H. Bunting was chaplain of our regiment and besides preaching and praying for us, one part of his work was to look after the mails—to send them out, receive them, and distribute them properly to the right parties. He also wrote regularly to the "Houston Telegraph" a letter to be published in that paper for information of our friends at home. This paper was published at Houston, Texas, and had a wide circulation in the State. In speaking of the battle of Farmington and its casualties in our regiment he wrote: "And the noble Blackburn fell at the head of the column, leading a charge upon the enemy." He never mentioned—and did not at the time he wrote know—whether I lived or died. My mother saw that news in the paper as soon as it arrived and after sitting some time in silence and agony of spirit she remarked to those present, "Well, if he had to fall, I am glad he fell at the head of the column, charging the enemy of his country." My sister who was present at the time told me of this remark, showing the patriotic resignation of our dear mother.

Let no one conclude that I or Company F was selected because of our fitness for the undertaking to lead and make this particular charge and to gain this honor, for many other companies in the regiment could have done equally well or better. It was a mere chance that we were at the front, as you will readily see when I explain to you that the companies on the march alternated in service at the front, taking the place in regular rotation one day at the front, next day in the rear, allowing next company to be front and so on until every company had taken its turn at the front. All scouts, messengers, and pickets were selected from front company each day, hence the necessity of changing and alternating regularly from day to day. This day of battle was Company F's day at the front, and as I was in command of the company this honor of leading the charge and bearing the brunt of the battle was thrust upon us.

My experiences as a prisoner of war were for the most part very agreeable and satisfactory during the time I remained in middle Tennessee, which was about one year. I was feasted by the neighbors in the town and good people from the country would send in town and take me out to the country for a week at a time as soon as I began to hobble around on my crutches. The young people insisted on my attending all the little gatherings they had, and as there were many nice young ladies on every side it was quite a pleasant existence for me.

After about four months' time when I knew I must soon face the ordeal required by one condition of my parole—to report to the United States forces as soon as I was able—I began to make preparations for it. First I asked Esquire

150

Reed, a strong Union man living in Lewisburg and man of influence with the Yankees, and a Mr. Idol Henderson, living at Cornersville a few miles away, with like qualifications, if they would accompany me when I went to make my report to the Yankees at Nance's Mills, just south of Cornersville, about one mile distant from there. They both consented very readily to do so. They had both been to see me and made my acquaintance and seemed to like me and sympathize with me, and I had an impression that they might be able to keep me out of prison for a while at least, because I knew that clause was intended to make me take the oath of allegiance to the United States Government or go to prison as soon as I could travel. So I set [out] the day before I could walk without crutches. Esquire Reed took me in his buggy and Mr. Henderson was to meet us at Major Evans's headquarters, who was in charge of Federal forces at that place. He was using Nance's Flouring Mills to supply the Federal army at different points in the State with flour and had a battalion of men, maybe more, about him for protection. We found Major Evans to be quite a nice man and a gentleman of quiet and friendly disposition.

We went in his office, and I presented my parole to him and told him I had come in to comply with the condition of parole, and while I was not yet able to walk without my crutches still I was able to report. Major Evans in a most jovial and affable manner said, "Why certainly, now let me administer the oath of allegiance to the United States Government to you, and as this country is full of pretty girls and a good country to live in you can have finest time a young man ever had anywhere." I shook my head and said, "No, I cannot do that." Then with a saddened expression of face at my refusal he said, "It becomes my duty to send you to prison." Up to this time my companions had not spoken, and I did not know what their plans were, for I had not discussed any plan with them, only asked them to accompany me. They said, or one of them said, "Major, we would like a private conference with you in the other room." The office was a two-roomed cottage with a stack chimney in the middle, with doors and shutters between rooms. For half an hour or more they consulted, leaving me alone with my thoughts. After a while they came in and Major Evans addressing me said, "Your friends seem to have much confidence in you." I said, "I am thankful, gentlemen." He continued, "They proposed if I would let you stay in the neighborhood that they would go on your bond for $10,000 for your good behavior, and I have concluded to accept their proposition." I said, "Many thanks, gentlemen,to you all." The Major continuing said, "The terms are agreed on. Who will write out the bond? Can you?" I said, "I never did write one and I had rather not undertake it." He then asked my two friends and his Adjutant too, I think. All asked to be excused and he said he didn't know how to do it himself, and seeming to be at a loss as to what he should do he turned to me and said, "If I release you on your parole without bond will you pledge your honor to behave yourself and abide by the other condition in said parole?" I said, "I surely will." He said, "Will you promise to report to me once a week so I may keep track of you and find you when I have to?" I said, "Yes, if you will allow a written report instead of a verbal one, as I have no means of transportation." So the agreement was made and I returned to my home at the McKnights at Lewisburg with a thankful heart, for I always had a mortal dread of prison life. This arrangement was satisfactory to the Federals and my parole protected me from molestation from the many passing commands I would see or meet almost daily.

I stayed at Lewisburg until some time in March, I think. I had made the acquaintance of a young Presbyterian preacher named Ewing, at whose mother's house I had been a guest a time or two. He had a monthly appointment to preach at Brick Church, about fourteen miles south of

Lewisburg, and asked me one time to accompany him down there. I accepted the invitation on condition I could get permission from Major Evans to do so. His route was right by Evans's camps, and I started with the hope that Major Evans would not object. He readily consented and I made arrangements to teach a little country school down in that neighborhood, where the people were trying to get up one. At Mr. Ewing's next appointment down there I went, carrying my scant wardrobe with me, bidding adieu to many kind friends at Lewisburg, whom I had become very fond of. I kept up my reporting to Major Evans on and on until some time in the fall.

General G.M. Dodge with a large force of Federals came to Pulaski, Giles County, and remained a while and was ordered from there on to Chattanooga, and took all the troops from that section with him, including Major Evans, and his command. It was said that the Major and his crowd got on a big drunk when they left that section. I know not how it was, but I do know that he went off without leaving me any orders, and now having no one to watch me I thought somewhat of my chances of going South and getting to my command and seeking a private exchange so I could take my place in my company. But the long trip seemed to be too much for me with one of my limbs still weak from the wound.

My school closed for a three month's term, and another one was offered me. I continued to teach for a while. One Sunday Doctor Gordon and I went to Cornersville to church to hear Dr. Stoddart of the Presbyterian Church preach. On our return home we met General John C. Starkweather, who had taken General Dodge's place at Pulaski, on the pike with one or two regiments of cavalry, making a reconnaissance up towards Cornersville. He immediately arrested us, made us turn back and escorted us and several other prisoners he had arrested back to town and to Esquire Chafin's office. He inquired of Chafin if he was a magistrate there and being told he was, he ordered him to enroll everyone of these men in the State militia as required by the proclamation of the Military Governor of Tennessee, Andrew Johnson, and then left us under a strong guard while the magistrate should enroll us in the service to help repel an expected invasion of the rebels from the South. I had made the acquaintance of a Mr. McBride who had deserted from a Texas regiment, joined the Yankees in that section and was acting as pilot or guide for Federal scouting parties who might need such help, and while I never saw him or knew him before, yet he seemed to take some interest in me, probably because we came from the same State.

Not long after we were put under guard, Mr. Stoddart the preacher came to me, asking the guard the privilege of speaking to me, and said in a very low tone of voice, "McBride says, 'What are you going to do?'" I replied in the same tone, "Tell him I am not going to enlist in the State militia." That ended our conference and he withdrew. A little later Stoddart returned and said, "McBride says for you to ask for a guard to take you before General Starkweather and when you get there you show the General your parole, telling him who you are and he will excuse you from the enlistment, he thinks." So I asked for the guard and he marched me up to the General's headquarters, holding a gun with bayonet on it in his hands behind my back all the way.

When I reached there, the General had just had a good dinner and plenty to drink and was enjoying himself talking and chatting with members of his staff. I pulled my hat off, walked in front of the General, saluted with a military salute, and stood before his majesty. He stopped talking, returned the salute, and waited to see what I would do. I told him I was a Confederate soldier on parole, was one of the men he had arrested and left with Esquire Chafin to be enrolled in the State militia and I had come to tell him that I would not be enlisted and asked the protection my parole guaranteed me. He asked for my parole and I showed it to him, and after a little consideration he said if I would report to him at Pulaski the following Wednesday he would release me and let me return home. I told him I would if there were no providential hindrances. So he dismissed my guard and gave me a pass to go home. When Wednesday came I asked Mr. Henderson to accompany me and he consented and I asked Mr. Lonnie Gordon to take me down and we three drove to Pulaski, went to General Starkweather's headquarters over on East Hill in Judge T.M. Jones' residence, and I presented myself before him saluting him. He didn't recognize me at first and I explained, "You arrested me last Sunday near Cornersville and released me with the injunction to report to you today and I am here according to promise." He still seemed in doubt. He pulled a memorandum book from his pocket, turned his back to me to get a better light on his book and began to look over a list of names he had on it. He commenced at the top running his finger along slowly—and said when half way down, "You say your name is Blackburn?" I answered, "Yes." He folded his book and remarked, "Major Alman gave me this list—a list of Confederates for me to look after." Major Alman, it is needless to say, was one of those Southerners who played both sides; always trying to curry favor with whomsoever controlled his section. Turning to me, he said, "Won't you take the oath of allegiance to the United States government." I answered, "No." He asked why. I answered, "I cannot swallow it and besides I owe allegiance to another government." He then said, "It is my duty to send you to a Northern prison." At this juncture my good friend, Henderson, asked for a private interview with the General. These two retired to another room and were absent for some time. When they came back I caught Henderson's eye and he slightly shook his head. I knew before the General told me that there was no hope in sight for me to escape the prison.

The General said my friend was good enough to offer to stand for me, but he couldn't be bothered with such things, and he would do his duty and send me on to prison. I said, "All right, but, General, it seems a long trip to make and a cold place to lodge for a man without a cent of money in his pocket." He agreed that this was true. I said, "General, I have one request to make of you." He said, "Say on." I said, "I have been teaching a little school where I live and I would like to have a few days before I start for prison to make some collections so I will not have to go without any money at all." He said, "If I will let you off for a week, will you report to *me* here at *Pulaski* next Wednesday?" I promised I would if the Lord was willing. He ordered his Adjutant General to give me and my two friends passes so we could go home, and this was the last time I saw General Starkweather, for before the next Wednesday came he obtained a furlough for sixty days and went up to his home in Ohio for a rest and recuperation. I hadn't promised to report to anyone except General Starkweather at Pulaski, so when the next Wednesday came I remained at home and didn't try to find him. By the time he returned from home, General Forrest who had taken Athens, Alabama, with about two thousand prisoners was marching up the railroad towards Pulaski, taking all the Yankee forces from stockades along the route and was now ready to lay siege to or capture Pulaski; and Starkweather was kept too busy to think of me. I knew he had returned, but as the time for my reporting to him at Pulaski had long since passed and no new date had been fixed for the report I simply didn't seek to have another day set for our meeting, and remained at home.

General Forrest after shelling Pulaski for a while didn't deem it prudent to make an attack there on account of the strong fortifications; then retired south and joined General Hood, now approaching Tennessee with his whole army. As the Southern army came in the State Federal forces in the

southern portion of the State retired before it and pretty soon
Giles County was under control of the Confederate soldiers
and I was again in the hands of my friends. I reported at once
to General Hood, gave him account of my history as a
prisoner, showed him my parole and asked him if he could
arrange for my exchange so that I might enter the service
again. He replied that he had a camp at Columbus, Georgia,
where he made private exchanges of prisoners with the
enemy, and he would furnish me with papers and transportation to that point, which would enable me to get the desired
exchange. So he issued the necessary papers of instructions
and orders for transportation on railway and for use of soup
stands for my benefit, and taking the papers I returned home
to make preparation for my trip. I purchased a fine mare
from Dr. Gordon which he had bought to use in his profession, but found he would be unable to keep her from the
raiding cavalrymen passing, often looking for and taking all
the best horses wherever they found them. He was very
willing to sell her to me for $125.00, taking my note for same.
My intention was to get in as good shape as possible and to
make the trip on horseback to Columbus, Georgia, and when
I got the exchange I would be mounted and ready for service.

While I was getting ready for the trip, General Hood
pushed on to Franklin, Tennessee, and had one-third of his
army slaughtered there, but held the battlefield and followed
the Federal army on to Nashville, where he was defeated by
the Federals, they being reinforced by another army.[15]
Before I was fully equipped for my journey General Hood was
falling back south with his army. So I delayed my start south,
to see if I would have company for my trip. A few days more
passed and Hood's army was passing through Giles County

---

[15] The battle of Franklin was fought on November 30, 1864; that of
Nashville on December 15-16.

going south. I fell in with the rear, far enough from the extreme rear to be out of reach of the continuous fire the Federals kept up on the rear guard of that retreating army.

The weather was extremely cold, many of Hood's army were entirely barefooted and ragged, and some of them wounded at Franklin were trudging along, making their way south to avoid capture and imprisonment. I never saw an army so dispirited, so needy, and withal so determined not to give up the contest. I had read of Washington's army at Valley Forge, barefooted and leaving a trail of blood as they marched over frozen ground, and I said within myself, "History is repeating itself before my very eyes." I traveled on and on and fell in with two more horsemen going southward and after dark came we looked for a place to stop for the night. I suggested that we get off of the main road for fear that some of these barefooted soldiers might find and borrow our horses while we slept. We turned east and went one-half mile from the main road, found a house where lived a family by the name of Marbutt and soon we were made welcome and comfortable by being housed and fed and having our horses fed and fine prospects for a good bed and a fine night's rest. Our horses were put in the smokehouse very near the house so that they would be safer than at the barn if anyone should undertake to steal them in the night, for there was much of that being done at this time. This was not very far from the Alabama state line, in Giles County, Tennessee.

Next morning on rising early I went to the smokehouse and found two of the horses gone, mine being one of them. Our saddles and bridles were undisturbed. We tried to trace them by following their tracks, but they had gone to the main traveled roads which were covered by millions of tracks of a passing army, so we had to abandon the search. I felt sure mine had been taken by some brokendown infantryman, who would think it fair to make me take turns with him in walking.

After our morning's search for horses had proved fruitless my two companions, one with a brokendown horse and
outfit, the other one with outfit and no horse at all started
out together to follow the retreating army, and I never saw
them again. I was left alone at Mr. Marbutt's to consider my
best course to pursue. I learned from some of the family, or
by observation I don't know which, that there was a blind
horse there in the barn, so I asked Mr. Marbutt if I could buy
him. He said he was blind and didn't see how he would suit
me, or really how he could do without him, but if I could
raise thirty dollars good money, I might take him. So I looked
over my finances and found I was short two and half dollars.
So I told Mr. Marbutt I had only $27.50 and would give up
every cent of it for his horse. He said it was a trade so I
handed him the money and took my bridle, saddle, and
blanket, and put on him and took possession. He was four
years old, good size, in fair condition, quite active, and not
a blemish or defect except he was totally blind. I rode him
all day following the retreating army until late in the evening,
when I began to look out for a lodging place for the night.
Houses were scarce and what there were in that section were
mostly vacant. It was fearfully cold and I felt that I must be
inside of some house or suffer greatly with the cold. I saw
smoke coming out of the top of a cabin about one hundred
yards from the road, and I rode up to it to learn the chances
of being sheltered for the night. I found five or six infantry
soldiers had taken possession of the cabin, which was
empty, had torn up the floor in the middle of the same, made
a fire down in the ground underneath, and were warming
themselves, sitting on the floor with feet down over the fire.
I asked permission to join them for the night. They readily
consented and I remained with them until morning, tying
my horse to the log house on the south side to protect him
from the cold, and he and I passed the night without supper
and next morning without breakfast.

The lady with whom I had boarded in Tennessee had fixed many things for my comfort and protection from the cold. Among other things a pair of heavy woolen socks to wear over my boots instead of overshoes, which were impossible to procure at that time. When we were dressing next morning, getting ready to move, a soldier remarked it looked hard to him to see a man with two pair of socks when he had none at all. I looked over the crowd a little bit and I saw they were all practically barefooted, so without a word in reply I stripped off those oversocks I had on, and handed them to the one speaking and said, "Gentlemen, I regret that I have not a pair for each of you." Next day I continued my journey south and coming to the Tennessee river late in the evening, I crossed over on a pontoon bridge prepared for use of the army. The following night I fell in with some cavalry of the 11th Tennessee regiment, the same being Captain Andrew Gordon's company, then commanded by Lieutenant James Edmundson, now living in Marshall County, Tennessee, about four miles east of Lynnville. I had been staying in the same neighborhood where many of this company were raised, and knew their families and kinfolks, so they made me entirely welcome and shared provisions and horse feed with me, making me as comfortable as they could. And now day after day I journeyed with the army southward, keeping a sharp lookout for my valuable black mare, but without success, finally reaching Columbus, Mississippi, where the army entrained for the East.

The exposure I had endured and change of diet and climate and habits, brought on an illness that kept me laid up for some days, when I found I had to go to bed for an indefinite period. I went out of town to a country doctor with a small family, with plenty of the world's goods and fair practice, who had been recommended to me, and applied to him for treatment and lodging for myself and board for my horse. He kindly took me in and cared for me some days until

I felt myself able to travel again. Then I told the doctor and family I must be off for Columbus, Georgia, my objective point; that they had been wonderfully kind to me, which I greatly appreciated, and that I didn't have a cent of money with which to pay them, but that I had a good blind horse there, saddle, bridle and blanket, all of which I would give them to pay for the care, treatment, and lodging they have given me. The doctor said that would satisfy him, and so we settled the debt and we parted good friends and everybody satisfied.

But I was completely strapped, only having now a little bundle of underclothing and a pistol, which a friend up in Tennessee had given me, and my journey was hardly begun. But I went cheerfully forward, thinking "A bad start may have a good ending." The Confederate government had established soup houses at convenient distances on the railroads to feed the soldiers in transit—I suppose for this particular army movement but I don't know. At any rate the train would stop two or three times each day for meals furnished free to soldiers. The meals were nearly entirely soup, pea soup or some other kind of vegetable in season at that time of year.

Nothing of especial interest happened until we reached Columbus, Georgia, after two or three days' travel. As soon as we pulled into the depot I asked the direction and road to the exchange camp, and with all the haste and speed I could muster, walked out to it, about one and one-half miles from town. When I reached there I found the place very well provided with shelter, bunks to sleep in with long dining tables and other things for taking care of prisoners, but entirely deserted except for a colored woman who was employed by the military authorities to cook for prisoners who were being kept for exchange. The cook announced to me at once that the prisoners were all exchanged and had gone and she was remaining there for a time to see if any more would be sent in. This was a sore disappointment indeed for me who had so constantly expected an exchange and freedom from further obligations imposed by my parole of honor.

I returned at once to town and hunted up the commandant of the post. At this stage of the Civil War the authorities had appointed at every principal city in the South a commandant of the post, and the whole country was under martial law and each particular section under the military control of the local commandant. I showed my papers, my parole and papers from General Hood, and told him of my disappointment. He expressed his regret and seemed to sympathize with me. We talked over current events for a while and the gloomy prospects of our army's success at that juncture, and after awhile he asked me what I wanted to do. I told him without hesitation and frankly I wanted to go to my command if he could tell me where to find it and could give me transportation. He replied, "Your command is now north of Savannah, Georgia, across the river in South Carolina, confronting General Sherman's army, which is getting ready to move up through South Carolina for her destruction, and if you want to go I will give you transportation wherever we have any. The railroads are torn up some places and you will have to do the best you can over those skips where there are no cars running."

So I made another start eastward on a train and I don't recall just how far we traveled before we had to walk. Another straggling soldier or two had fallen in with me by this time, all trying to reach their command further east, and they walked with me for miles, ten or fifteen or more. Now a new trouble overtook me. One of my wounded limbs having not gotten sufficiently strong for the journey began to fail and I had to let my late companions in travel leave me alone, so I rested and limped on and on as well as I could until I passed over the gap. The soup houses had given out now, and I had to depend upon strangers in a strange land for support.

One night I stayed in a neatly built log house, two or three women and some children living there alone. I remember they used what they called "light'ud" for illuminating purposes. They seemed to have plenty of plain food to live on and some to spare. I recall a conversation occurring at the table at supper. The lady of the house asked me where I was from. I told her "Texas." She said, "Well, well, from the far Texas." I said "Yes." She replied that she always thought she would like to live in Texas. After a little silence she asked me if we had any "light'ud" there. I said not in my section where I lived, but in other sections there was plenty of it. She remarked she would not live in any country where there was no light wood.

Now my journey was one of variations, sometimes on a railroad, sometimes on a wagon going my way, and sometimes afoot; but I continued with a firm set purpose to reach my command and finally succeeded in doing so, somewhere in the southern part of the State of South Carolina. My comrades rejoiced at my return to them. They were all so blackened by pine smoke it was difficult to recognize them. My heart ached when I inquired for many with whom I soldiered in former times, when the response would be dead, or disabled from wounds, or disease and discharge. My comrade Street, with whom I left in charge my $250 mare, my saddle, blanket, spurs and pistols had been killed on a hazardous scout and my belongings had fallen into the hands of the enemy when he fell. Many changes had taken place. Officers to fill vacancies caused by death, discharge or promotion were no longer elected by the men, but went up by virtue of seniority of rank. My old captain had been promoted to be major of the regiment, leaving the captaincy in the company vacant, and awaiting my return to fill it, as I was next in rank in the company. The second lieutenant, A.J. Murray, was in command of the company.

I reported my arrival to Generals Wheeler and Hampton, then commanding all the cavalry forces in South Carolina, showed them my parole of honor and gave them the details of my efforts to get exchanged and of my travels. They commended me for abiding by the terms of my parole and told me to remain with my company and they would arrange for a private exchange for me, so I could take charge of my company again.

Now commenced with me a new experience in my life. There were no wagons now belonging to the cavalry to carry their cooking utensils and camp equipage and to afford a safe refuge for the non-combatants as formerly, but each company had a pack mule upon which was carried the frying pans for the company and a soldier or a negro cook to lead the mule during the day, following the company constantly except when engaged in battle. An oil cloth was used instead of bread trays, and a flat rail or board used for the baker, and when a rail or board was not available a limb cut from any tree was trimmed up and held over the fire with dough wound around it to cook. The potatoes, the only abundant article of food to be had, were roasted in the fire. I ate and slept with the company, and when the battle came on I was herded with this frying-pan lead-horse crowd until the firing ceased. This was the most disagreeable experience I had during the war. I urged the officers to hasten the exchange if possible, and so they offered to exchange a major of Kilpatrick's staff for me; but General Sherman refused to do it when he learned what command I belonged to, remarking, as I heard, if he had any one of that command fastened he would not release him for anyone, and so I had another disappointment. Now it is proper and fair to tell why General Sherman should refuse to swap a Texas Ranger for one of his own men of higher rank.

Captain Shannon had become chief of scouts for the Southern army, and he and his command were Texas Rangers, or most of them were, and were known as Texas Ranger scouts; and they became quite efficient in killing Yankees without capturing any they found burning houses or insulting women, which was the daily habit of Sherman's men as they marched through South Carolina with torch, rapine and devilish lust. General Sherman in retaliation for what the Texas Rangers were doing and had done put sixty prisoners in irons and threatened to execute them. General Hampton heard of this threat, sent a flag of truce to Sherman for a conference with a view of saving the lives of those prisoners in irons. General Sherman complained that the acts of these Rangers were not in accordance with the rule of international warfare, but uncivilized butchering. General Hampton's reply, as I now remember the published reports of the conference at the time, was that he had observed all rules of international or honorable warfare, but when his antagonists engaged in burning down the houses over the heads of women and children, and non-combatants, without provocation, and in insulting and raping the helpless women of the land, he would order his men in all such cases to kill without mercy everyone so engaged and if he wished to retaliate by executing prisoners, he (Hampton) would enter the same game, taking two of Sherman's men for every one Sherman executed and in every case giving his (Sherman's) officers the preference.[16] General Sherman saw his bluff could not be carried out for the reason, perhaps, that twice or three times as many Yankee prisoners were captured daily as were taken from the Confederates, for our scouts were exceedingly active, being on all sides of the enemy almost daily, while the Federals were straggling all out from the main body, trying to desolate South Carolina, because they

[16] This correspondence may be found in *Official Records*, Series I, Vol. XLVII, Part II, pp. 546, 596.

regarded her as exceedingly wicked in being the first State to secede from the Union. The irons were promptly removed from the prisoners and they were sent in to our camps without the formality of exchange. These poor fellows came into the camps full of wrath against the Rangers for their murderous acts and said, "You men think it fine sport, but if you had to take our chances as hostages you would play the game differently." But their wrath and injunctions were wasted on their audience, for the Texans were fully decided as far as possible to protect the honor and property of helpless people against the vandalism and destruction of an unprincipled antagonist, whose main ambition seemed to be to make the Southern people realize that war was hell as their leader was accustomed to say to them. Just what there was in the truce conference held to cause the release of the prisoners may be only surmised, but why General Sherman refused to make the exchange sought seemed manifest at the time to parties most interested.

The ravages of war were fearful to behold. Any one could stand upon an eminence in the morning and tell by the smoke from burning buildings just how far east and west General Sherman's line of march extended. From the daily reports, which we believed authentic, every living animal for use or food was taken from the citizens, including all kinds of fowls, and their smokehouses and pantries were stripped, and when the women and children would appeal to General Sherman for food he would tell them to call on their people in the northern part of the State. There was just one article of food they could neither destroy nor carry off and that was sweet potatoes, of which there was an abundant crop the season before which must have been the means of keeping the dependent population from starvation.

Of all the campaigns made during the Civil War by either Northern or Southern armies, none had more of devastation and cruelty and inhumanity than this one led by W.T.

Sherman across South Carolina, during the winter and spring of 1865. And no other campaign equaled this one for its barbarity except perhaps Sherman's march from Atlanta to the sea. After his army reached Savannah, Georgia, Sherman made his report to the Secretary of War, in which he said he had made Georgia realize that war was hell and that he had devastated a country fifty miles wide and two hundred miles long so completely that if a crow visited that section he would have to carry his rations with him or starve. This report was published at the time and is now doubtless among the war records today.[17]

This incident will probably bring to the mind of the student of history how Nero fiddled and danced while Rome burned up. Sherman left Atlanta with an army of between fifty and one hundred thousand men for his campaign through Georgia and the Carolinas, opposed only in Georgia by Wheeler's cavalry, reinforced by other cavalry forces under General Hampton, McLaws and other local commands when he started through South Carolina, not enough at any time to resist his progress materially, but enough perhaps to delay his movements somewhat while he repaired the bridges destroyed by the Confederates and enough to keep his men reasonably closed up in solid columns and thus saving from destruction some of the districts near his line of march. This marching of Sherman's army accompanied by the burning of houses in the country and of the towns and villages passed, and the general destruction of property continued without variation or cessation worthy of mention until he reached the capital of the State, which shared the same fate as other towns in the line of march.

But at this juncture General Sherman published a report

---

[17] For Sherman's account of his march to the sea, see his *Memoirs* Vol. II, pp. 171-229; also *Official Records*, Series I, Vol. XLIV, pp. 7-14.

in the papers that General Hampton had burned Columbia; and while no soldier in either army in South Carolina believed it, yet there were others who did give that published report credit. Of this latter class was one, writing in Nelson's Encyclopedia, who in speaking of this destruction of Columbia said, "The charge that he ordered the burning of Columbia, South Carolina, has been completely disproved," leaving the impression on the reading world that Sherman's charge against General Hampton was true. It seems strange that one who presumes to write history should be so careless about facts. Now why should anyone conclude that a man who had spent months in destroying and burning everything in a devastating campaign should be relieved or exonerated of the charge of burning Columbia, the goal of his ambition and cherished conquest of his military career. Besides this process of reasoning, to fix the blame on General Sherman, I have seen published a report that I deem reliable, that General Sherman published in his memoirs before he died that he charged General Hampton with burning Columbia in order to discredit him with the people of South Carolina, his native state. I have never seen those memoirs and cannot vouch for the truth of this report, but it seems reasonable and much in keeping with General Sherman's character.[18]

John G. Haynie of Company F, as good a soldier as ever Texas sent to war, was drowned in Saluda river at Columbia the same day the city was burned. Haynie had rarely ever missed a battle, had been wounded two or three times, and had no hope or expectation of ever going home again, as he confided to me only a few days before his death. I asked him why he should take such a gloomy view of the future. His answer was, "This war may last ten years, and I am not going to shirk a duty or miss a battle if I can possibly help it; and

---

[18] This confession is in Sherman's *Memoirs*, Vol. II, p. 287.

I know it is only a matter of a short time when everyone who does this way will meet his final call. Judge the future by the past. Look for the best soldiers of Company F. Where are they? Most of them have answered their last roll call, and I can't hope for a different fate."

While Sherman was making desolate these regions the army of Tennessee was collecting in North Carolina near Raleigh or rather in that section of the State, for the purpose of meeting Sherman's march northward. General Joe Johnston, who had been succeeded by General Hood at Atlanta, was restored to the army of Tennessee while said army was near Smithville, North Carolina. I never saw a demonstration to equal that made in honor of his return. Nearly a whole day was consumed by the army in cheering and shouting over this event. The army had nearly been destroyed by Hood's manipulation of it, and the remnants were wholly dispirited by the misfortunes that had befallen our cause, and having great confidence in General Johnston as a leader and successful warrior, they showed renewed enthusiasm and determination by the magnificent reception accorded him.

A week or ten days later General Johnston moved his army out to meet Sherman in his onward march and met him at Bentonville, North Carolina, and engaged him in battle which lasted two days, March 19-21, 1865. It was furious and bloody from the beginning and to a spectator it seemed that the Confederates had the advantage on all parts of the field. I had no special duty to perform, being on parole. I was exposed several times to the enemy's fire when I ventured too near to watch the battle or to help carry the wounded from the field.

During the first day the Texas Rangers lost. In the first charge they made every field officer they had, Colonel Cook, Lieutenant Colonel Christian and Major Jarmon, was badly wounded. In after years Cook died from his wound. The other two recovered after the war ended.

Doc. Mathews, a mere boy, captain of Company K, being senior captain now with the regiment succeeded to the command of the regiment and won unperishable fame by making a successful charge on the 17th Army Corps of the enemy, driving them in great confusion from a bridge they were ready to seize. This bridge was the only available crossing of a deep sluggish stream around our army on its west and south sides, and in case of its capture by the enemy in front our army would have been cooped up and forced to surrender. Our ammunition and supplies had to come to us over that bridge. The enemy fully realized the importance of its capture and approached near to it without being discovered, with a whole corps of infantry. The Rangers, being the nearest Confederate troops to this point, were ordered by General Hardee, who was nearby reconnoitering that part of the field, to drive them back. With a charge rarely equaled and never surpassed in impetuosity and daring, the Texans under Doc. Mathews' leadership threw themselves upon that corps of infantry with a recklessness that indicated do or die on their part. The enemy were greatly confused and wavered for a moment and then began to give back. The Texans still pressing were reinforced by Brown's brigade of Tennesseeans, I think, and the two commands combined drove the enemy clear off the field and the bridge was saved to us for our use.

The toll of the Texas regiment was heavy in the killed and wounded, but the charge was a success, as most of its charges were. It was reported that General Johnston said he would compliment that regiment in a general order, but owing I suppose to the great confusion in military quarters and the fast changing of operations just previous to final surrender, the complimentary order and the official report of this battle were never written so far as I know. This was the last battle of the Tennessee army of any consequence.

In this last charge General Hardee had a son killed, about 17 years of age. The boy had been in military school at Milledgeville, Georgia. The dash and success of the Texas Rangers challenged his ambition. He left school without permission, came to the army, sought out the Rangers and offered his services in their ranks. His presence and desires were made known to General Hardee who sent him back to school at Milledgeville. He made his escape from school again and came to us during the battle of Bentonville. He was again reported to General Hardee by Captain Kyle of Company D of the Rangers. Hardee said to Kyle "Swear him into service in your company as nothing else will satisfy." Kyle enrolled him in his company. About four hours after this time this fatal charge was made and he fell dead in sight of his father, who had come out to see the charge made. Of course I cannot recall many of the casualties that happened in that battle, but one other case is so fixed in my memory that I feel constrained to mention it.

Eugene Munger of Company B of the Rangers had escaped the missiles of death so long, not even receiving a wound from the enemy, though always in the thickest of the fight, that he had become a fatalist, and often said that he didn't believe a Yankee bullet was ever molded to kill him. In that charge a bullet went crashing through his brain, and he never knew what killed him. So much for fatalism, so much sometimes in presentiment. I have known other cases where these things failed in realization.

One other thing in connection with this famous charge. General McLaws from the Virginia army witnessed it. He said he had soldiered with "Jeb" Stuart on his many exploits in Virginia and Maryland, but had never witnessed a charge equal in efficiency and results to this one.

The great battle of Bentonville was now over, both sides badly punished. Sherman's hitherto unimpeded progress was checked, and he gave his time and energy to recruiting and repairing his army, and General Johnston to organization and moving leisurely towards Greensboro, North Carolina. In the meantime the Virginia army was surrendered at Appomatox, and General Grant's army moved south to make a junction with Sherman's army and to force the surrender of General Johnston which finally took place at Greensboro. Just before the armistice between the two armies, Johnston's and Sherman's, took place, one other incident of interest might be related pertaining to the Texas Rangers.

They were camped out on Haw river, or some tributary of it, near a bridge over a stream. Pickets between them and the enemy had been removed during the night without their knowledge. Next morning about sunrise a regiment or more of the enemy's cavalry came across that bridge into the edge of our camps, while all the regiment were asleep except five or six men who had saddled their horses to go out for forage. These raised a shout, made a dash at the enemy, thus awakening the balance of the regiment, who instantly grabbed their guns without any orders; everyone for himself, and gave them such a reception as to send them pell mell back the road over which they came. So far as I now remember this was the last firing by any part of Johnston's army, and so the Terry Texas Rangers had fought the first and last battles of the army of Tennessee; the first at Woodsonville, Kentucky, the last near Haw river, North Carolina.

Not long after this Captain Doc. Mathews, now commanding the Texas Rangers visited General Hardee's headquarters to learn what he might about the current events of the day. General Hardee was a favorite of the regiment, and the regiment was a favorite of his. He told Mathews of the situation pending; that Grant was moving upon us from the north and Sherman's army had approached us from the south and east, and General Stoneman had 10,000 cavalry on Catawba river southwest of us, and that while he had nothing official on the subject, he felt satisfied the army would be surrendered right there. He also advised Mathews to take his regiment away from there and join Dick Taylor's army then at Mobile, Alabama, and by thus adding strength from different sections of that army, under the providence of God victory might finally come to the Southern cause, and added, "I don't want to see your regiment surrendered to the enemy."

Captain Mathews returned to camp at midnight and had the bugler sound the assembly call for the regiment, and when it was assembled he delivered Hardee's information and advice and concluded his remarks with these words, "I am too young a man to assume the responsibility of such an undertaking, but I now offer my resignation as commander of the regiment," asking each company commander to take charge of his company. "Hold a council to determine your course, and each company decide and act for itself regardless of what others may do."

Company F, my company, returned to quarters, held its conference and decided unanimously to go to Dick Taylor and to start at once. Some of the company, including the commissioned officers, were absent on police or scout or other duties or on account of sickness, and were not in this conference and hence were left behind when we started to leave. C.D. Barnett, our orderly sergeant, agreed to be commander and I agreed to be "counselor" for the expedition. I never did learn definitely the course the other companies pursued, but had the impression fixed upon me that most of them made their escape and were never paroled until after all Confederates had surrendered, and some of them were never paroled at all, but are still, so to say, soldiers of the Confederate government. Some parties, making out as best they could a roster of the regiment, since the war, in speaking of this surrender of the troops said that two hundred and forty-eight Rangers answered to roll call the day before the surrender, but only two of them surrendered next day. I think this is erroneous, but indicates how much the Rangers opposed surrendering to the enemy. Captain Tom Weston, last commander of Company H of the Rangers, wrote to me some years after the war closed and said among other things that he had the honor of surrendering the regiment at Greensboro, and that there were ninety men present who received paroles. I think this statement is reliable.

About fifteen or eighteen members of Company F at one o'clock in the morning began their journey south for Mobile. We went through Greensboro. Brigadier General Harrison of our brigade heard of our movement and sent for us to come to see him, where he was laid up with recent wounds received in battle, and when we drew up in front of the house, he came out on his crutches and made us a speech. He commended our movement heartily and regretted only that he was unable to accompany us. Then with many tears and benedictions he bade us Godspeed with God's blessing and a loving farewell to his faithful comrades who were, according to his words, the heroes of 300 battles.

From Greensboro we went the most direct way to Catawba river. We employed a guide to show us a private ford, knowing that all public crossings were heavily guarded by Stoneman's cavalry. Our guide rode with us all night and towards daylight we left the main road, took a by-path which took us to the river by sun-up where our guide pointed out to us the ford, telling us we would have to swim twenty or thirty feet in the middle of the stream, and ascend on far side up a little trail leading up the bank. Thus instructed we dismissed our guide and moved forward. Having crossed the river and ascended the bank we found a cabin up on the bank and a lane leading out to the main road, which ran up and down the river two hundred yards or more distant.

Soon after leaving the cabin we saw about twenty Yankee cavalry coming in the other end of the lane meeting us. They were some of Stoneman's men patroling up and down the river to intercept Confederate soldiers trying to make their way south. I was in the rear of our company, which halting for a moment asked me what to do, I said, "Move forward quietly and when within ten steps of them raise a yell and charge them with your pistols in hand and demand their surrender." They were surprised at the unexpected charge and surrendered without firing a gun. Now with twenty prisoners, well mounted, and well armed, we moved forward at a lively gait, crossed the main road, went through the woods, fields and pastures, until we had many miles between us and Stoneman's command. We traveled on and on, going south until nine o'clock at night, when we began to feel the need of rest, and began to consider what was best to do with our prisoners, I suggested to my men to take their horses, arms and munitions, parole them, and turn them loose to return to the command afoot, so building up a fire of pine knots, the paroles were soon written for each one and signed up. We then took possession of their horses and equipage, bade them good-night and we moved on several miles further and camped.

Next day we continued our travels south, taking from Confederate commissaries and quartermasters' stores in the towns we came to such food and feed as we needed. The officers in charge of such stores sometimes objected, saying that Johnston's army had surrendered and that they had been ordered to turn over these supplies to Federal authorities. I gave them choice of opening their storehouses where provisions were stored or having them broken open. They unlocked them and told us to help ourselves. I told them after they had supplied the Confederates' wants they might turn over the residue to Federal authority; that we were regular Confederates and were eating Confederate food and using Confederate forage.

Not many days later we learned that General Taylor had

surrendered his army[19] to Federal authorities without a single battle, and we were confronted with new difficulties. Another council of war or of procedure was necessary on our part, so we decided to turn west and cross the Mississippi river by private ferries and offer our services to General Kirby Smith commanding the Trans-Mississippi department. Still another difficulty arose, for we had now reached that desolated strip which General Sherman's army had made on his famous march to the sea, and it was exceedingly difficult to obtain supplies for a company of men. We then divided into squads of three or four men in each, with the promise to meet on the east side of the river to reunite there and go in a body across the river to General Smith's army. Being separated into smaller bodies we more easily found subsistence. Thus we all traveled westward on widely differing routes. As we began to gather in Mississippi, still a new obstacle to our progress was presented. We had hoped to use canoes or skiffs in crossing the river, swimming our horses beside them, a custom that prevailed in that section after the public crossings had fallen into the hands of the enemy. This could be done when the river was at its ordinary stage or depth very successfully; but now what was termed the June rise was on, caused by the melting of ice far up North and the spring rains, and the river was thirty to forty miles wide, making it impossible for our mode of crossing for a month at least, perhaps more. So we must await the falling of the waters before we could cross over.

While lying up and waiting Tom Gill, Peter Arnold, John Justice and I concluded we would take a run up into middle Tennessee, where we all had sweethearts whom we desired to visit. So after forging some paroles for Justice, Gill and Arnold we made our start for Tennessee. Now I don't wish to

---

[19] May 4, 1865.

make the impression that I forged these paroles for the boys, for I did not, but they found other men on parole down there in Mississippi and copied them substituting their own names in place of the one on parole. Thus equipped, well mounted, and armed with our side arms we started for Tennessee. As we approached Wayland Springs in Lawrence County, Tennessee, we unexpectedly at a short turn in the road rode into a regiment of Yankee cavalry who were dismounted and seemed to be resting under some trees by the roadside. We halted for a moment and I said, "Forward, boys, and look for the commander of these troops." So pretty soon Colonel Blank was pointed out to us by the troopers and we rode boldly up to him, all of us saluting, when Tom Gill became spokesman for us, and said, "Colonel, we are Confederate soldiers on parole, going up farther in Tennessee to visit our friends before we proceed to our homes in the West." In the meantime we all drew out our paroles for the colonel's inspection, and Gill continued his speech, saying, "You see, Colonel, we have our side arms. These are for our own personal protection, as Federal officers in Mississippi advised us that if we came to Tennessee we would find bands of outlaws, horse thieves, etc., plentiful, and we ought to have some defence against these."

After examination of two of the paroles, the colonel bade us to proceed on our journey.

This was about six or eight miles south of Wayland Springs, which was the regular camping place for this regiment, as we learned later in the day. These springs as it happened were on the road we were traveling. After sundown as we approached these springs that evening, a sentinel on guard called out to "Halt! Halt!" several times, to which we paid no heed, but kept riding on towards him. When we drew near this sentinel was furious and cursed us vigorously and threatened to shoot us. His calling to us and cursing us aroused the curiosity of his comrades back in camp, so they, eight or ten of them, came out to the road to see what the trouble was. They first discovered we were Confederate soldiers, and one discovered we were on McClellan saddles and said, "Why, they are using our saddles," meaning we were riding saddles the Federal army used for their cavalry, and then another one called out, "Why, they are armed with pistols; look at them." Then I said, "Yes, we have our pistols and all of us know exactly how to use them, so you need not trouble yourselves further about trying to halt us, for we are going on," and bade them good-night, and rode on. It may be but fair to state that they had come out to the road without their guns and as the vidette only was armed and we had two six-shooters each, they simply acted wisely and judiciously by letting us pass on, without molestation. This was my last personal interview with the Yankee soldier.

Next day we reached Giles County, and as some of the crowd wished to go on up to Franklin County and on to Maury County while I wanted to stop in Giles County, we separated with the understanding we would meet at my stopping place to begin our western trip after the Mississippi river had gone down sufficiently. Pretty soon, after this date, Generals Lee, Johnston, and Taylor, having surrendered, the future for our independence seemed so unpromising to General Kirby Smith's army that they simply broke camps and went home without awaiting any enemy to ask them to surrender. So their final act in this fearful drama was called "The Breakup" and is still so-called.

In our last contact with the Yankee troops down in Lawrence County I did not endorse Mr. Gill's speech to them, for it was only one-fourth correct, since I was the only one that had a genuine parole, but he proceeded on the theory, I suppose, that "all things are fair in war."

The war was now over, our dream of an independent Confederate government was passed. Overwhelming numbers with inexhaustible supplies had triumphed over a half-fed scantily supplied army, greatly inferior in numbers. I am reliably informed that war records of this period will show to parties seeking correct history that the Confederate enrollment of soldiers was 600,000 in all, while the enlistment on the other side was 2,800,000, or more than four to one in favor of the Northern army. In addition to this, all Southern ports were blockaded by the Federal government, so it seems wonderful even yet that this war could have continued four years with this great inequality of advantages.

Personally I had been loyal to the Confederate government, had done the best I could, had offered my life, endured privations and shed my blood freely; had no apologies to make for my action, and still believed and now believe we were right and engaged in the cause of human liberty as did our forefathers in other years. I do not know certainly, and do not want to know how many men I killed or how many I wounded. I only know I had many fine opportunities to do both. I wear four scars on my body from Yankee bullets that will go with me to my grave, but I regard them as scars of honor received in defense of the Southland, and am proud of them. I thank God that I can forgive and pray for my former enemies and that I entertain no ill will towards any of them at this time.

In the foregoing pages I have in a plain way told where I served and when I served in the Confederate army, together with many incidents connected therewith. I have tried at all times to be accurate, and fair and loyal to the truth. It now remains for me according to first intention as announced in the beginning of this record to tell just why I served the cause with such fidelity. I might answer this question with one word "Patriotism." I believed the South right in her contentions and in her actions in seceding from the government and setting up for itself. According to the Constitution, Amendment X, the powers not delegated to the United States by the Constitution nor prohibited by it to the States were reserved to the States respectively. These independent States never delegated their powers to make or unmake governments to the general government, so if they ever had the right of choosing in this matter and had not delegated it to others, they still possessed it. These independent Colonies, or States, had never lodged in the hands of the general government the right to make war on any one of its members. Secession it was said was advocated by Abraham Lincoln in a speech in Congress as a right belonging to the States respectively. Massachusetts threatened secession when the government purchased Louisiana from France, because, as her people argued, the price paid was extravagant. Fanaticism in the Northern States caused them to pass fugitive slave laws in violation of the Constitution, in Article IV and latter part of Section II, and when reminded of this violation the usual answer was, "The Constitution is a compact with the Devil and in a league with Hell." They brought on war and bloodshed in Kansas because some United States citizens had moved to Kansas and took their slaves with them, as I now remember. The same fanaticism sent emissaries through the South to raise insurrection among the blacks, and to incite them to bloodshed and murder and when one of those was condemned and hanged for his murderous deeds, those fanatics held great public funerals over the North, proclaiming him a martyr to the cause of human welfare and to the holy service of God.

In addition to all of these things this same element increased in strength and power until it was able to elect a President and a Congress of the U.S. from its members and what could the South expect but humiliation and destruction of her institutions from such a set?

The time had come when we believed we could not live peaceably with them. Therefore, we preferred to secede and form a government of our own, which we thought we had a right to do. We did not demand any of the public treasure or public lands or any of the community property of the government of which we rightfully owned a part, but simply seceded from disagreeable company and set up a government of our own and asked only to be let alone. I doubt if a constitutional lawyer could have been found at that time who would have said we did not have a right to secede and I doubt if you can find a constitutional lawyer today who understands the organic law of the government who will say that we had no right to secede. Then where did this power lie or come from authorizing Abraham Lincoln to make war on and devastate the Southern States?

There is another viewpoint that justifies the South in going to war. Self-preservation is the first law of nature and a people who would not fight to defend their homes and firesides are not worthy of freedom or respect. I love the South and her institutions and I went out to help defend them and to help if possible drive the destroyers from our borders, and old as I am now, if such a catastrophe should happen again to our beloved land, I am ready to offer my life, my fortune, and sacred honor in her defense.

CONCLUSION

It is self-evident from the foregoing writings in these sketches that if the writer were asked to fix the responsibility of the Civil War he would say, without hesitation, Abraham Lincoln, his ill advisors and coadjutors were responsible for all of the bloodshed, the deaths, the horrors and devastation of that war. But as another Judge, the Judge of all the earth who will do right, has jurisdiction over these and all other human affairs, the writer is willing to leave these and all other things for Him to adjudicate.

Terry Ranger Monument,
Austin, Texas.

The Terry Texas Ranger Monument on the grounds of the state capitol in Austin, Texas. The surviving comrades of the Rangers had this monument erected in 1907. The granite base is topped by a fourteen foot bronze statue showing a Ranger with his rifle at the ready. Pompeo Coppini was the sculptor, and Lucas & Meir the builders of the monument.

Plate 18

William H. Jones served as
Second Lieutenant with
Company A. He was wounded
at Mossy Creek in December
1863 and after recovery
became an enrolling officer at
Camden, Alabama.
Plate 19

Thomas M. Jack served as a
private in Company B until
1862 when he became an
aide to Gen. Albert Sidney
Johnston. At war's end he
was a Colonel and
adjutant-general of the
Texas District.
Plate 20

*William Andrew Fletcher
served initially with the 5th
Texas Infantry before
transferring to Company E of
Terry's Texas Rangers in
March 1864. His
reminiscences of service with
the two units was privately
published in 1908.
Plate 21*

*George W. Littlefield enlisted
with Company I in September
1861 serving first as
Sergeant, then Lieutenant
and Captain. He was
wounded in the battle of
Mossy Creek in December of
1863 which led to his having
to resign in June 1864.
General Harrison is said to
have promoted him to Major
of the regiment for gallantry
during the battle of
Mossy Creek.
Plate 22*

Walter H. Caldwell enlisted in
Company D in 1861 and
served until the end of the war.
Wounded in September 1864 in
a skirmish in Northern
Alabama.
Plate 23

Thomas P. McCampbell
served initially with the
Eighth Tennessee Cavalry
before transferring in March
1863 to Company G of
Terry's Texas Rangers and
serving until the end
of the war.
Plate 24

Edwin M. Phelps enlisted in
Company G in 1861 and was
promoted to Lieutenant in 1863. At
the end of the war he was serving
as acting adjutant of the regiment.
Plate 25

William Reuben Webb enlisted as a
private in Company B in September
1861. He was captured near
Somerville, Georgia, in January
1864 and imprisoned at Rock Island
Barracks, Illinois. He was
exchanged at New Orleans in May
1865. Plate 26

James Foster McGuire was a private
in Company D from March 1862 until
June 1865.
Plate 27

Rufus Y. King, Lieutenant, then
Captain of Company A in October
1861, was wounded at Shiloh and
resigned in August 1862. Plate 28

DIARY OF EPHRAIM SHELBY DODD

Member of Company D
Terry Texas Rangers
December 4, 1862 - January 1, 1864

Five Terry Texas Rangers of Company C pose in their varied dresscoats but with the uniformly distinctive star on their hats. Bunting wrote that E.S. Dodd was wearing this distinctive "Terry's Texas Rangers" hat when he was captured.
Plate 29

INTRODUCTORY NOTE

In his history of "Terry's Texas Rangers," Mr. L.B. Giles narrates the following tragic incident of the East Tennessee campaign:

> "It was during this winter that one of the saddest events in all our career happened: the hanging of E.S. Dodd by the enemy. He was a member of Company D. He was of a good family and well educated. For many years he kept a diary, setting down at night the happenings of the day. He was taken prisoner with his diary in his pocket. On that evidence alone he was condemned and executed as a spy."

In January, 1914, the State Librarian received a letter from a resident of New York State, informing him that she had in her possession a diary found on the body of a Texas Ranger hung as a spy. Negotiations for its acquisition by the State Library were opened at once, and terminated successfully. The only information about the diary this person could give was that it "was found by a lieutenant from a N.H. regiment, who for years was a friend of our family, and some time before his death (which occurred six years ago) he gave it to me."

E.S. Dodd came to Texas from Kentucky late in 1860 or early in 1861. After visiting an uncle, James L.L. McCall, at

Waco, he made his home with another uncle, Dr. John R. McCall, at Austin. He was teaching school near Austin, and was not yet out of his teens, when he enlisted in Terry's Rangers.

—Ernest William Winkler
Texas State Library
November 5, 1914

DIARY OF EPHRAIM SHELBY DODD

Transferred from old Diary.

Thursday, December 4th, 1862—I went out from M. to Mr. ——, five miles from town. I went from there to Gen'l Morgan's Headquarters, leaving the Knox county filly at Mr. — and riding Walker's horse. I took supper at Lewis Black's, Morgan's Headquarters. The Gen'l was in town but came in just after supper. I went on to Chenault's camp and staid all night with John and Van Benton.

Friday, 5th—Snowed all day. I rode to Alexandria and went out to Mr. Bass', seven miles, got there about night. I found all well.

Saturday, 6th—I remained quiet to-day. Miss Frances came over. I staid all night and Sunday, 7th, I started on my return to camp. Came to Statesville, got pair of boots, $25. Came out three or four miles and staid all night.

Monday, 8th—I got some cloth and came to town (M.); stopped but a short time. I saw Miss Kate, received a nice present, a sack to carry tobacco, made of red, white and blue. I came out to Mr. House's and staid all night.

Tuesday, 9th—Came back to camp. Company on picket. Burke in command at camp. I was put on comm. guard.

Wednesday, 10th—Lieut. Ellis went on a scout. I went with him. Ten men detail went down on Wilson pike, turned off to left and staid all night with Mr. Smith, a clever man, nice family, daughters, etc.

Thursday, 11th—Crossed the railroad and went down near Franklin. Got a guide and went down country through farms, etc., to near Brentwood, stopped at Miss Mag. McGarrock's. Came back to Mr. Campbell's, two miles from Franklin, and staid all night.

Friday, 12th—This morning just at daylight, while in the act of eating breakfast, the fight commenced in town. We put out immediately; found the Yanks in possesion [*sic*] of the town when we got there. Their pickets fired on us. We then crossed the creek to go round and get with Smith. Got into Mr. Baugh's lot and while there came near being surrounded by a hundred or two Yanks. Came cross country to Hillsboro, got good dinner and came back to F. by night. Yanks left about 11 o'clock. Found Smith in possession. Came out two miles and staid all night.

Saturday, 13th—Came back to Camp. I went on forage.

Sunday, 14th—Got a good dinner at Mrs. T.

Monday, 15th—I and Jeff Burleson went out and got a good dinner and my clothes. Came back and found the Company in Camp. To-night I, Eslinger and Jessy Johnson went out cross the hills to preaching. Parson Bunting officiated. I went down with Eslinger and the girls to Mr. Page's, got some good apples, set till bed time and came to Camp.

Tuesday, 16th—Remained in camp.

Wednesday, 17th-Saturday, 20th—During this time had several false alarms amounting to a run down the pike and back to Camp. Also regular turns on picket.

Sunday, 21st—Go on the famous detail to M. after guns which cost me three days' roots. I went to see Miss Kate, spent about three minutes, had to make flying visits. Called to see Mr. Lane's family. Coming back to Camp, stopped to get supper and did not get to Camp till after night.

Monday, 22nd—Put on three days. A false alarm caused

us to go to the front.

Tuesday, 23rd—Went on picket. I was put on at the Widow....

Wednesday, 24th—Was transferred to Black's picket at Holt's and stood to-night.

Thursday, 25th—This morning just after being relieved the Yanks made a break on us. We were fired on just as we reached the Com., fought them all day, falling back about four miles (Christmas Day). Returned to Camp.

Friday, 26th—Were aroused early this morning with the word the Yankees are in Nolensville. Went up at double quick and found them there. Fought them there all day until night, falling back to our old Camp at Mr. Page's. Staid there to-night. Our loss, one piece of cannon and a few men— McClure of Company E killed.

Saturday, 27th—Commenced skirmishing early, falling back slowly; fought through Triune and beyond Mr. Perkins. Rained on us all day. After passing Mr. P's, we took up line of march, came up three miles and turned off for Murfrees-boro. I stopped and spent the night in a kitchen; came on Sunday 28th and overtook the Regiment. We came in five miles of M. Met the wagons, unloaded them and prepared to cook three days' rations, but were ordered to saddle up and get out to meet the Yankees. A false alarm. Staid out until near midnight. Came back to where we left the wagons but they were not there.

Monday, 29th—Went out this morning to the end of the Wilkerson pike. Met the Yankees and skirmished with them all day, falling back gradually. Their cavalry charged us once but paid dear for it. A number of prisoners were taken. We fell back to our infantry this evening.

Tuesday, 30th—Rained to-day; all quiet till evening; fight then opened between the infantry and continued until dark.

Wednesday, 31st—The great day of battle commenced at daylight and raged heavily all along the line until 3 o'clock.

Yanks drove back four miles. Our Boys took in prisoners by the hundreds. Captured twelve cannon and during the day about 2000 prisoners, 160 odd beeves, some wagons, etc.

Thursday, 1st January, 1863—Went to La Vergne and pitched into their wagon train, captured and burned a good many wagons, 200 prisoners.

Friday, 2nd—Transferred to the right wing. Saw the fight this eve. Breckinridge had to fall back. Raining all the time.

Saturday, 3rd—Raining all day; sent out on a scout last night beyond Stone River to Mr. Black's. All quiet.

Sunday, 4th—This morn before day our Army commenced to retreat. I left the Regiment on the Plaza in M. and went out to the end of the Wilkerson pike. Got my clothing and came across to the Salem pike, found a number of unparoled Yanks on my way. I met Gen'l Buford but he would not send back to parole them. I went on to town, went to see Miss Kate, took a bite to eat and bid them goodbye. Went up to Mr. Lane's and from there out to Col. Smith's Regiment and back to Col. Cox in town. He promised to attend the Yanks. I then started for the Command. Came out to Col. Lytle's, stopped, found Morton of the Battery there. I took supper there but did not know where I was until the young ladies came down. Miss Mollie came in glad to see me, was then introduced to Miss Mollie Turner and Miss Alice Hord, staid till 11 o'clock, time passed very pleasantly. Came on to Camp.

Monday, 5th—Fell back to Old Fosterville, remained 6th-10th.

Sunday, 11th—Came out on a reconnoitering expedition, past Col. Lytle's. I stopped on return and saw Misses Mollie and Alice. Miss Molly T. had returned home. From this time until the 27th we did nothing but picketing. I piruted a little on Duck River, spent a night or two with Mr. Stewart, took dinner twice at Mr. Wilhoit's and thus the time passed. On 27th came in to Camp and on 29th we were relieved by

Wheeler's Brigade and with three days' rations started on a scout down on Cumberland, passed through S. and out on Eaglesville pike to E. Camped near the place.

Friday, 30th—Came through Triune and out to Franklin, got there 4 p.m., went out one and half miles on Columbia pike and camped. I and Oly Archer went out to Mr. Baugh's and took supper, staid till bed-time and returned to Camp.

Saturday, 31st—Details sent out to get all the provisions possible and return by 12 o'clock. I went to town, but did not get my horse shod, met the command as I went out, coming in. Went some ten or eleven miles and camped on creek on steep hillside. Rained all night. I and John Henry slept dry in my Yankee tent. Most Company got into stable and crib.

Sunday, 1st February—Rained all day, came within four miles of Charlotte. A very poor country. I and Reuben Slaughter went out and staid all night with Mrs. Hood. Her husband had been conscripted. She boiled a ham, baked some pies, filled our haversacks and started us on our way rejoicing. Came down to Mr. Ventress.

Monday, 2nd—Froze up and snowed to-day and night.

Tuesday, 3rd—Started before day for Fort Donelson. Had to walk to keep from freezing. Got to the Fort about three hours by sun. Our Regiment sent on Fort H. road to prevent reinforcements from coming to D. Reached our position and the fight commenced and continued till dark. We cut the telegraph at all points, fight resulted in capture of about 100 prisoners, 50 negroes and same number of horses, one twelve-pound brass rifled cannon. Gun Boats came up after dark and commenced shelling and we had to get. Came back to the Forge, two and a half miles, and camped.

Wednesday, 4th—Came back to Ventress's on Creek. Snowed to-night—awful time.

Thursday, 5th—Boys had grand snowball. Gave Col. Harrison a taste. Came up Columbia road, twenty miles, to little village of Wharton, took up quarters. We went up creek three miles and back close to Headquarters and camped in road, making fires of the fence. I got fodder and we spread it on the snow and blankets on fodder; slept comfortably.

Friday, 6th—Came to Vernon and camped. I went out and got some fodder and made beds, but did not get to enjoy it long. Bout 1 o'clock started and came to Duck River, built fires of the fence on river bank. Our squadron sent on scout eight miles, got back just after day. Found them swimming the horses and taking the rigging over in a boat flat. We were then sent on picket. A ford was found and the Brigade crossed over. Camped one mile from the river. Crossed near Centerville.

Saturday, 7th-Sunday, 8th—Came up to Columbia pike, ten miles from town. Once more in pretty country. Camped in woodland blue grass pasture.

Monday, 9th—Moved up in five miles of Town.

Tuesday, 10th—Remained in Camp.

Wednesday, 11th—Sent to Headquarters to draw ammunition as A.O.S. Gen'l Wharton had a ball to-night.

Thursday, 12th—Came up to within seven miles of Lewisburg.

Friday, 13th—Came up to L. I went with Aeron Burleson to the fortune teller's; had our future destiny read to us; then to Mr. Lane's and listened to Miss Jennie paw ivory awhile. Miss Mattie Long present.

Saturday, 14th—Remained quiet today. I and Nix went to see Miss Jennie Lane. Miss Mattie still there.

Sunday, 15th—Moved camp out seven miles on Franklin pike near Berlin. I went out to Mr. Sewell's and got dinner; piruted around and came back to Camp with two dozen eggs.

Monday, 16th—I went our piruting again to-day. Wagons got in to-day. I was put on Camp Guard; roots for being out. Soon after dark a detail was called for to go to Lewisburg; 'twas raining; I was detailed. Doak in command. Got there about 11 o'clock, could find nobody, went into Court House and slept in the Bar.

Tuesday, 17th—Received twenty-four boxes, saddles, bridles, halters, etc. Sent to Camp. Got a detail and put them all in a house and locked them up. We took charge of the Clerk's Office to sleep in, tied our horses in Court Yard and got our forage from the farmers around. Secured boarding at Maj. Holden's, a clever gentleman and nice family; has one grown daughter, Miss Emma, a nice young lady. Remained here Wednesday, 18th-Monday, 23rd. During this time had nothing to do but write letters, visit MY GIRL THAT PAWS IVORY, and make acquaintances. Among them Miss Lou Hill I prize highest. We had prayer meeting and church. I purchased four books and left them with Miss Emma: Mormon's at Home, Pilgrim's Progress, Bayard Taylor's Travels and Bible Union Dictionary.

Tuesday, 24th—Just before leaving a couple of young lady equestrians passed out of town from Mr. Fisher's. I jumped on H. Emnoff's horse and overtook them, rode out a mile with them and turned off pike. If I should ever get back to L. I intend seeking them and make their acquaintance. After dinner we bid our kind friends adieu and put out, overtook the Command about eleven miles from Shelbyville.

Wednesday, 25th—Came through Shelbyville to-day. Commenced raining on us just as we got to town and continued. Came out on road to Beech Grove, ten miles, as wet as water. I and Albright went cross Wartrace Creek and staid all night with Mr. Fork—a nervy layout.

Thursday, 26th—Still raining. Went over to Mr. Hancock's, intending to cross Wartrace at a bridge above but gave it out as it was pouring down rain. Found Charley Pellam there at Mr. H's.

Friday, 27th—All start this morning for Camp, find the wagons close to Fairfield, the Regiment three miles further on. I was sent after corn over the highest mountain in the country as soon as I got in.

Saturday, 28th—Moved Camp out near Beech Grove. I and Polk Kyle sent on forage, bought a stack of hay. Staid all night with Mr. Carlisle.

Sunday, 1st March—Got his wagon and hauled one load to Camp. Camp moved three miles further up the pike. I went up Creek and got Mr. Jonichin to start with his wagon. Went on top the mountain to get two more wagons and as I came back the Yanks ran our pickets in. I came near being caught by them. Came back down Creek and told J. He turned back. I and Polk then went on to Camp. After going to bed, all waked up and fell back to the other Camp.

Monday, 2nd—I and Polk go out again. Get Mr. Ashley's wagon and Mr. Carlisle's; send in two loads. Camp moved up pike again. Go into Camp.

Tuesday, 3rd—Company went on scout. Unshod horses did not go, so I staid.

Wednesday, 4th—Company on picket. All gamblers and pirutes put on roots. I came under the latter head.

Thursday, 5th—Still on picket.

Friday, 6th—Relieved by K. and F. Raining all day and night. Sent on bread detail with Big Ugly, got back after night, raining.

Saturday, 7th—I went out to Widow Ewell's to get some bread. Regiment relieved and went into Camp. I got there after night.

Sunday, 8th—Went on forage; got back in time for preaching.

Monday, 9th—Remained in Camp to-night. Rained.

Tuesday, 10th—Could not get forage.

Wednesday, 11th—Went after forage. I and Reuben Slaughter went together, did not find the Squadron, piruted around and came back to Camp after night.

Thursday, 12th—Came (Regiment) down through Shelbyville to near Dolittle. I stopped at Lee Stewart's and got dinner. Came on to Camp.

Friday, 13th—Went on bread detail, saw Mrs. Billington at Widow Clardy's, her mother; took dinner with them. Met Miss Ore and Miss Patton.

Saturday, 14th—Squadron went on scout. I went to shop and on bread detail.

Sunday, 15th—Remain in Camp.

Monday, 16th—Last night had a meeting of the Lodge; passed two and raised one; made the acquaintance of Dr. Moore and lady, also Miss Stern, a niece of the Doctor's.

Monday, 16th—Another meeting; one passed and two raised.

Tuesday, 17th—I listened to some delightful music this morning by Miss Stern, particularly the Texas Rangers, dedicated to Mrs. Gen'l Wharton. I started back to Camp but met the Regiment going out on picket. I fell in and went out and had to come back or go back and get my blankets. Came out half a mile from D. and camped.

Wednesday, 18th—Remained in Camp all day. I am very unwell.

Thursday, 19th—Came on picket this morning.

Friday, 20th—Our Squadron sent on post this morning. I joined Tom Taylor's mess; Jessy also. I and Tom went out to Mr. Elmore's and got some bacon and milk. I stood to-night.

Saturday, 21st—Brigade went out on scout. Our Company supported battery, drove the Yanks back to their main camp and returned.

Sunday, 22nd—Parson Bunting preached for us to-day. Nothing occurred to change monotony of camp. Sick, and time drags slowly with me.

Monday, 23rd—A false alarm to-night, and rain.

Tuesday, 24th—In Camp—quiet.

Wednesday, 25th—Roll call five times a day, arms and

horses inspected in the morning and dress parade in the evening is the order of the day.

Thursday, 26th—Drill two hours and dress parade. A document from Gov. Lubbock of Texas read, giving an account of presentation of flags of 4th and 5th Texas Infantry of Virginia to the State. Also one or two captured by our Regiment.

Friday, 27th-Monday, 30th—Nothing of importance occurred.

Tuesday, 31st—Went on a scout out to Eaglesville. Met a Yankee scout just this side of E. We charged them and run them one and a half miles, capturing six and wounding several.

Wednesday, 1st day of April—Yanks brought up three or four thousand to E. and shelled our Boys for some time.

Thursday, 2nd—Went out beyond Maj. Winn's, brought his family and negroes out, skirmished with the Yankees for some time, nothing serious.

Friday, 3rd—I went out piruting this evening, came back to Camp and went in to Dr. Moore's, sit till bed time. Miss Nannie made some music for me; the evening passed pleasantly.

Saturday, 4th—The Grand race between Wharton and Harrison came off this morning. All the Regiment that wished to went out. I remained in Camp. I and Reuben S. went over and got dinner at Mrs. Blanton's. Came back and the Regiment was getting ready to leave. I and Lonnie Logan came on to town and stopped at Dr. Moore's. Miss Nannie made some music for us. We bade them goodbye and overtook the Regiment. After we got to Camp, I took John Rector's horse and went up to Mr. Stewart's; found Dan at home. I took supper and staid all night; got some provisions fixed up and left before day. Came down to Camp and started soon after up country.

Sunday, 5th—I came by Dan's and got my clothing,

overtook the command at town. Came up to Fairfield, crossed Bell Buckle Creek, went three or four miles and camped.

Monday, 6th—Came up near Jacksboro and camped.

Tuesday, 7th—Marched on way to Liberty far enough to consume the day when we turned back in getting to Camp; had to go down and up a pretty steep mountain. The Yankees had possession of Liberty, drove Morgan's men out. We came back to Ballou's (Blues) and camped. Nothing for our horses to eat or ourselves.

Wednesday, 8th—We came down to the forks of the pike two miles from Liberty. I and Reuben Stroud stopped and got supper and our horses fed. Found four companies on picket, ours among the number.

Thursday, 9th—I, Tom Taylor and Stroud came on to Alexandria and shod our horses. The Regiment passed on and left us. We came on and got our dinner at Mr. Neal's living near Mrs. Grandstaff's and came on to Camp at Spring Creek.

Friday, 10th—I was very sick last night and hardly able to ride this morning. Command left before day, got to Lebanon at daylight. Dr. Hill could not get the medicine for me but gave me a pass to return to the wagons. Near McMinnville I came out to Mr. Bass's and staid all night.

Saturday, 11th—I felt better this morning but very weak. Francis came over this morning or evening. George Tracy was over in the morning, I believe.

Sunday, 12th—Rained last night. Very pleasant this morning. I remained quiet to-day. Three or four soldiers came by; found our Brigade had come back about Spring Creek.

Monday, 13th—My mule taken scratches or something else badly, cannot ride her. Pretty day to-day. Aunt Nancy came over this evening.

Tuesday, 14th—Rained last night again and cleared off

this morning. I remained quiet to-day. Rained again to-night.

Wednesday, 15th—'Twas misty and damp this morning. I fixed up and went up to Mrs. Tarpley's, bidding the folks goodbye at Mr. Bass's. I found the way pretty easy. Killed a squirrel and took dinner with them. Staid an hour or two and started; came on through Commerce and out two miles to Mr. Davis and staid all night. The mist finally turned to rain.

Thursday, 16th—Cleared off this morning. I remain with Mr. Davis to-day; very pleasant day.

Friday, 17th—Lieut. Davis and Emmet Trammel came by to-day and took dinner. Learned all about the Regiment from them. Camped at A. To-day was a beautiful day. I did not feel so well as I have for a few days before. Fine time for farmers to work.

Saturday, 18th—Hermosa mañana. Nothing unusual occurred this morning. I passed most of my time reading; still gaining in strength.

Sunday, 19th—Rained last night; beautiful spring morning this. Rained again all morning till 12 o'clock and cleared off.

Monday, 20th—I leave Mr. Davis this morning for Camp. Go out by Rainey's. I got my cartridge mended and came up to Mrs. Grandstaff's and got my dinner. Came on to A.; met the Regiment just at Camp, on their way to Lebanon. Our Squadron on picket. Sent after them. As soon as they came Regiment started. Got to Lebanon about 11 o'clock. 'Twas two before the last of the column passed. A train of wagons was along after the Com's. We stopped on street and the train passed on. We picketed all the roads and remained. I slept on street, my head resting on curbstone for a pillow, but one blanket and got very cold before day. At daylight I went down and washed my mule off and warmed in blacksmith shop. Started back and Ferrill being drunk had me arrested. Kyle had me lay off my arms, but soon after Regiment all went to water and I was released. I eat breakfast and went over to Mr. Davis. Cousin Mec and Miss Fannie were at home. Mr. Davis down in town.

Tuesday, 21st—I remained in town some two hours. Went over to Camp, moved my mule to where 'twould be safe in case of a move and went down to Mrs. Jordon Stokes. I had a good long conversation with her. Got a paper from her and just as I was leaving Kyle came in. I loaned him the paper and went over to Cousin Mec's to take dinner. Hank Sullivan came in after dinner. Fox Trammel and Jim Davis came for dinner. The Miss Thompsons, sisters, came in. I went into the parlor with Hank and was introduced to them. We then had some music. An hour or two passed rapidly. We took leave. I promised to call again in the evening. I went over to Mrs. Stokes and after making addition left a letter which she kindly promised to send to Nashville and mail for my Father. I got some more papers. She and Mrs. Muirhead, her mother, tried to make a proselyte of me to Lincolnism or Unionism, as they would term it. Commenced raining. We left soon after I got back; came out near Cherry Valley and camped. I was on picket; the Reserve in a barn; the Videttes in a blacksmith shop; a good time of it.

Wednesday, 22nd—Rain ceased; bright and clear this morning. We came on to Alexandria. I spent the evening working with my mule's feet. After supper I went over to Lodge to assist in conferring some side degrees. I took 1001; staid till 11 o'clock. Came back and went to bed. In a few minutes ordered to saddle up. Yanks coming down on us like thousand of brick from Liberty, Snow Hill and all around. We marched all night. I and Jack and Bill Kyle got together. Couldn't keep up with Regiment. Stopped at daylight, got breakfast, fed horses and traveled on. Crossed river—nearly swimming. Came out three miles and camped.

Thursday, 23rd-Friday, 24th—Remain in camp this

morning, all day nothing of interest.

Saturday, 25th—Start at 3 o'clock for the wagons at Yankeetown. All horses unfit for duty sent there under Lieut. Gibson of 11th Texas. Regiment went to Rock Island. We came in fifteen miles of Sparta and camped. Men and lame horses straggled all along the road for miles. I and McFarlan bunked together.

Sunday, 26th—Came on by Mr. England's; stopped on Mountain at Mrs. Lowe's and got some bread baked and duck cooked; took dinner and came on to Camp. Found the wagons camped near Yankeetown.

Monday, 27th—Remained in Camp all morning; then started as John Rector had come in to see Cousin Jim Hawkins; found he had moved camp. I went up to Mr. Johnston's and took dinner; saw Mr. Denton of Mike Salter's Company there. Sent note up to Jimmy by one going up.

Tuesday, 28th—James Hawkins came up to-day to see me; staid all day with me. After he left, I and Frank McGuire went out to Mr. Bradley's and got supper. I got some bread. We then went and got twenty bundles fodder apiece and came back to Camp.

Wednesday, 29th—Remained in Camp to-day; horses inspected. John R. left me to go to the command. Albright bunked with me to-night. I went up with him to Mr. Williams and got supper.

Thursday, 30th—Came up, I and Albright, to Brown's Mill. Regimental wagons ordered to Sparta. Regiment on detached duty; spent night with Cousin James Hawkins.

Friday, 1st day of May—Spent this day with Jimmy.

Saturday, 2nd—Went to Granville. I rode Jimmy's gray horse and left my mule with his boy. Staid all night with Capt. Trousdale; had to paddle over the river in a canoe and swim our horses.

Sunday, 3rd—I went on by Duke's and to Squire Bennett's on Buffalo Creek. Took dinner and remained till near night. Then crossed the pike at Hogg's Store and up to Billy West's and spent the night.

Monday, 4th—Came on to Abel Smith's and to Widow Ballou's and took dinner. From there to Womac Parker's on Dixon Creek, and staid all night.

Tuesday, 5th—Came to Gifford's blacksmith shop. Albright had swapped horses, had two shoes put on, got dinner and came on to Joe Carter's. A. had two more shoes put on, went on to Griggs and got supper. A. and Maze of Petticord's Company came on. We came four miles to Joe Sullivan's; left A. there. I and Maze went over to Jordan Carr's. Yanks all through here yesterday.

Wednesday, 6th—Left Carr's and came up to John Mitchell's. Came out to Stinson's on to Giles Harris. From there to Scottsville and Gallatin. Crossed at Coatstown, went on to John Rippy's, got supper and fed horses. Went on in rain to the Webb's, Maze's uncle, found the Yanks so close by that we turned and went back to the hills.

Thursday, 7th—While at John's, Green Crews and John West came in. I went with them over to Mrs. Dinah Huffey. A. soon came, said Yanks were about. I staid all night. He went to John West's. Miss Polly is a fast one.

Friday, 8th—I went to John Mitchell's to meet A.; was not there. I went on to John West; saw Miss Jane Wiley; came back to D's; found A. there. I came back to John West, and on to Dots Belt's; staid all night; on to Green Crews this morning.

Saturday, 9th—Start this evening, six of us, to Allen County, Ky. Went up in eight miles of Scottsville; stay all night or day in woods. To-night go by Ayres, Will Span's and old man Span's. At the latter place we got into hot water. Bushwhackers attacked us, killed my horse, stampeded all. I got separated from the rest, went one mile, got two horses, came on through to New Row Monday, 11th, and on across to Coatstown. Find Will at Mrs. Huffey's, shot. Miss Sallie

Key there on visit. I stay all night.

Tuesday, 12th—I and Will Rogers went over to Green's and Bass's; met by John M. Green getting in. Met Albright, went back to D's and stay all night. S.K. there.

Wednesday, 13th—I met some of Morgan's men; Harper with them. I joined them and went cross railroad at Mitchellville over to Wickwire's, eight miles from railroad. Stopped at Mr. Simpson's and got breakfast. Miss Sue Offutt, Miss Jimmy Wickwire there. After breakfast went to the woods and staid all day.

Thursday, 14th—This evening we all went in and got supper then down to Mr. Wickwire's and got supper and the supper is a mistake; danced until 12 o'clock. I and Miss Jimmy danced two sets. I enjoyed it finely, then bid them adieu and came out to Pete Laurence's by daylight. Birch swapped horses on the way. Pete's sister brought us provisions.

Friday, 15th—To-night stopped to see two Lincolnites; got six shooter from one, single barrel from the other; stopped at Squire Henry's; got some cherry bounce; played off Yankee on him; got all the information we wanted and went on to Wickwire's; fed at Mr. Simpson's; girls got up, chatted them awhile. I, Harper and Gibson then left the crowd, crossed the railroad and bought two horses and came on to Bracken's and got breakfast. From there to Ashlock's and got dinner. Came cross the pike and I left them, went by Bass's and on to Crews and staid all night.

Saturday, 16th-Sunday, 17th—Came to Mrs. Huffey's, found Albright.

Monday, 18th-Tuesday, 19th—Yesterday went to Tompson's Shop; not at home. This morning to Hughes; gone to Gallatin. Came by Jordan Carr's, got dinner and on to Moss's. Found Jim Berryman there. Harper came soon. Went down to Sullivan's, fed and I left. Went on to John Stewart's, staid all night.

Wednesday, 20th—Down to Hughes, got my horse shod, came back, and nine of us started. Came up near Epperson Springs, found the Yanks were there and at Scottsville too strong for us. Got supper at Stinson's, a regular tory. Lamb swapped horses with him. Then started for New Row. Came across to Bracken's, got breakfast, three of the boys had left us.

Thursday, 21st—We came this evening out to where the others were; Yanks in New Row; so we could not go there. Came to Widow Hodge's. Five of boys went on; two slept in bushes; I and Jim Berryman slept in house.

Friday, 22nd—Came cross the pike to Meadows, fed our horses. I, Jim and Lamb started back to Kentucky. We came cross pike to Mr. Hodges and got supper, then cross railroad and out through Mitchellville to Norris ten miles from railroad; staid all day and to-night.

Saturday, 23rd—Went down to Finche's and got a horse. Mr. Finch came out with us some distance. Came back to Norris; staid all night; nothing to eat.

Sunday, 24th—To-night went down near Redman's; run into Yankee pickets, and started back. Came cross railroad and out to Sherwin's, got breakfast and on to Boss Meadows. From there to Hughe's Shop; got two shoes and nails made. Went down to Essick's and got supper and on top Mountain and staid all night.

Monday 25th-Tuesday, 26—This ... got my mare shod, went on, found A. at Henry Mitchell's came back to Hardy Silver's, found the boys and started back to the railroad to get some boots. Took supper with Mr. Hodge and on to Rodimore's; had not the boots; then came back cross pike. I went with Berryman to shop; Hughes not there. I left him, came on to Jack Stewart's. I, Albright and Lamb started back for Granville this evening; came on to Griggs, got supper. From there to Staffords and staid all night.

Wednesday, 27th—Met Thompson's and Staley's men.

Thursday, 28th—Came to Montgomery's. Lamb left us. We came on to Widow Ballou's. Yanks close at hand. We staid in bushes to-night.

Friday, 29th—Went to Dixon Springs to-day to get a Yankee saddle; had to wait until the two Regiments of Yankee cavalry and train passed out. We then went in, I and Ward. I went up to Mr. Alexander's; Miss Mollie knew me, Miss Nannie did not. I took supper and staid till 10 or 11 o'clock and left. Came back to Mrs. Ballou's.

Saturday, 30th—Came to Mr. Beasley's and staid all night.

Sunday, 31st—Met up with Parker as [and?] Lieut. Brown. I got a horse for Mason Rector. Came on to Granville, found Company D. there, and that we were published as deserters. Came out near Cookville to-night.

Monday, 1st day of June—Came to Mrs. Brown's, took breakfast, got our clothing and came on to Camp. Camp moved this evening. Proceedings stopped until Kyle comes up. Our names sent with others to be published in Houston Telegraph. Came out to-night to pasture and turned in.

Tuesday, 2nd—Came in to Camp, find that my name has been sent on with others to be published as a deserter.

Wednesday, 3rd—Ordered to remain in Camp.

Thursday, 4th—Wm. Hamby got in from Austin, Texas; staid all night with me. We went out to a private house and spent the night.

Friday, 5th—William left me this morning. To-night I and Reuben went out to Mr. Mills and staid.

Saturday, 6th—Lieut. Black took all men able for duty and started to Sligo this moring. To-night the Company got in from G.

Sunday, 7th—Started for left wing, went to Sparta, halted there hour or two; came on to Cany Fork and camped.

Monday, 8th—Came to McMinnville this morn. Ordered Regiment to Hoover's Gap to picket; wagons to Manchester.

I went to the wagons to get a saddle, stopped with Dave Nunn, staid all Tuesday, 9th. Came to camp, rigged my tree and Wednesday, 10th, came to the command, camped near Beech Grove on pike.

Thursday, 11th—Came on picket.

Friday, 12th—On picket duty; camped at our old stand.

Saturday, 13th—Company go on picket.

Sunday, 14th—I and Capt. Hill go out after provisions, stop at Mr. Mankin's, Prayters, Jacob's, Mankin's and return.

Monday, 15th—I took dinner to-day with Mr. Guess. Relieved this evening. Five of us went on scout; got supper at Mr. Mankin's. I left my valise at Mr. Guess's. I forgot to note leaving undershirt and pair of drawers at Mr. Brown's on Falling Water.

Tuesday, 16th—Regiment relieved and came into camp.

Wednesday, 17th—Drill morning and evening inspection. Received two letters, one from Cousin Jennie, one from Tom Maxwell.

Thursday, 18th—Review of Brigade by Gen'l Hardee.

Friday, 19th—Regiment came to Fairfield and from there to Bell Buckle and camped. I went out to Mr. Suggs and got some bread baked and returned.

Saturday, 20th—Remained in camp to-day. Three of the Arkansas Post boys came up from Wartrace and among the number was Doc. Norwood. Staid with us to-night.

Sunday, 21st—Came over to Old Fosterville to picket.

Monday, 22nd—All quiet.

Tuesday 23rd-Wednesday, 24th—Company on picket. I came back to attend a court martial; staid all night in Camp.

Thursday, 25th—Rained all day. Yanks made a general attack on our pickets. I went out to the Company about 11 a.m.; fell back to Ransom's; went over to Bell Buckle; traveled all night. Came on to Fairfield; staid a short time and came on back to Ransom's and camped.

Friday, 26th-Saturday, 27th—Came to Bell Buckle this morning and from there to Wartrace, our infantry falling back to Tullahoma. Went a short distance beyond Wartrace; 11th Texas and 4th Georgia skirmished with them a little; a few wounded. We came to Duck River and camped.

Sunday, 28th—Came on to-day to Tullahoma; continues to rain night and day. I saw James Maxwell, Billy Dunson, Julius Lensing and Doc. Norwood.

Monday, 29th—I was detailed to go to the shop; came on to town, found Stroud and came out five miles to shop. Still raining. We spend the night at the shop.

Tuesday, 30th—Our work finished and we return to Camp at Tullahoma. Regiment came in soon after. I got a letter from Miss S.A. Jourdan. I went over to the Texas Brigade, saw Doc. Norwood, George Holman, George Jourdan, Frank Wilkes and Billy Dunson. Came back and our Regiment moved out on the right and camped. I went on a scout with Black to Hillsboro; went within one mile and came back; no Yanks there. Traveled all day or I should have said all night. Got back and found the Army on the retreat.

Wednesday, July 1st—Army in full retreat. Came on to Alisony bout 11 o'clock. While on the move from that point my mare fell and broke her left foreleg just below the knee. John Henry was left with me. We came on short distance and went to sleep. I left my mare where the accident happened.

Thursday, July 2nd—Came on to Deckerd this morning. From there took wrong road and came up Cumberland Mountain to the University with Hardee's Corps. Found there that we had taken the wrong road. John went down to the house to get some information and I lost him. I came down to the railroad and staid all night. Polk's Corps crossing all night.

Friday, 3rd—I waited until our wagons came up and put my luggage on them and rolled on. Came to foot of Mountain to-night.

Saturday, 4th—Came down to Battle Creek from head of Sweden's Cove; portion of Polk's Corps crossed pontoon at mouth of Battle Creek and cross the river. We came on to Bridgeport. Crossed this evening. Met Bob Ship here.

Sunday, 5th—Came up to the foot of the mountains and camped.

Monday, 6th—Start cross the mountains. Came up, I and Paul Watkins, to Nicka Jack, staid all night with Mrs. Porter.

Tuesday, 7th—Came cross the mountain through Hamburg, got dinner there at Mrs. Reeves and came on to Camp within one and a half miles of Trenton.

Wednesday, 8th—Remain in camp.

Thursday, 9th-Saturday, 11th—All quiet. Put on one month's roots for the Kentucky trip; read at dress parade yesterday evening; commenced this morning.

Sunday 12th—Start this morning for Rome, Ga. Came on top Lookout Mountain; rained to-night.

Monday, 13th—Came on through Lafayette and six miles beyond. I and Bob Ship, Tom Peterson and Jim McGuire stayed all night about one mile from Camp. Rained very hard for a while. Music to-night.

Tuesday, 14th—Came to within fifteen miles of Rome, passed through Chanyville.

Wednesday, 15th—Came to Rome; pretty place for the Country. Camped two miles from town and spent all day in town.

Thursday, 16th—Remain in camp all day.

Friday, 17th—All quiet in Camp. Brigade officers had a ball in town last night.

Saturday, 18th—Moved camp down on Silver Creek four miles from town.

Sunday, 19th-Friday, 24th—Usual routine of camp duty. A protracted meeting going on, conducted by Parson Bunting and others, commenced Sunday. I am on duty every other day[.] Weather warm and dry.

Saturday, 25th, to 1st day of August—All quiet; usual routine of camp duty. Two days since, while out on forage, I saw Miss Anna Ransom at Mrs. Garrett's—a great pleasure to meet with them.

3rd, 4th, Wednesday, 5th—The barbecue and presentation of the horse to Gen'l Wharton came off to-day. Jno. Rector made the presentation speech. Gen'l W. replied. Harrison made a few remarks; dinner was then announced. After dinner Billy Sayers and Adams of Company C made speeches. Everything passed off finely; quite an array of beauty present. The Misses R. and G. present. I paid my respects to them.

Thursday, 6th, to Friday, 14th—Nothing but roll call, inspection, dress parades and drill. We are living high on peach pie. I have made a few acquaintances, but don't find the hospitality that we did in Tennessee. I was over at Mr. Bryant's to-day. Can't say that I enjoyed it very highly.

I pass from 14th to 20th. Nothing stirring. Oh! yes, the wedding—Charley Littlefield to Miss Mollie Maddry, by the Rev Mr. or Lieut. Simpson of Company B alias Sim Bruce of Company E. My time passes very pleasantly.

25th—Went to town to-day. Passed the day pleasantly; took dinner with ... Rome. Saw Cousin Millie; came out to Mr. Mobley's; took supper. Met with Col. Cox, Mr. Barrick of Glasgow, Ky., and Mr. Johnson and Lady of Nashville. Miss Mobley was very sociable. I sit till bedtime. Time passed pleasantly. Now, that we are acquainted, have become attached to the folks, we have to leave; always the case. I made the acquaintance of Miss Maggie Ezzell, Miss Mattie Sommers, Miss Fannie Summers and Miss Mollie Robert and enjoyed myself with them finely.

Friday, 28th—We bid our friends adieu and came out eight miles above Rome. I got my hunting shirt as I passed through town, cost me sixty-eight dollars.

Saturday—Remained in camp.

Sunday 30th-Monday, 31st—Moved four miles this evening. I and Jim McGuire went out and spent the night with Mr. Anderson.

Tuesday, 1st—Came on to-day to Mrs. Partain's where we stopped as we went down; found Mr. Sewell there still mending clocks; the girls looking charming. Staid all night. Music and mirth.

Wednesday, 2nd September—Came on to Lafayette, camp one mile from town. Had a meeting of the Lodge this evening; I attended.

Thursday, 3rd—Remained here to-day; met again this evening at the Lodge in town.

Friday, 4th—Started for Alpine; came out twelve miles and camped.

Saturday, 5th—Reached Alpine, left one wagon to the Regiment, and with the rest the dismounted men started for Rome. Came eight miles and camped.

Sunday, 6th—A number of us started at two o'clock this morning and came on twelve miles and got breakfast. I and Oly Archer turned off at Coosyville and came by Miss Ransom's. Miss Anna and Miss Fannie were there, also Mr. and Mrs. Settle of Murfreesboro. We spent the day with them and came to camp in the evening.

Monday, 7th—Camped at Col. Shorter's; one brigade of infantry near us.

Tuesday, 8th—All quiet. I went off over to John's last night, but big Cousin was not there.

Wednesday, 9th—Quiet to-day.

Thursday, 10th—I went over to Whitehead's to get some raw hide to cover my saddle. I stopped at Mr. Mobley's and took dinner, chatted Miss Metta a while and went over to the Mill and on to the tan yard and back to the Mill; found Dr. Neely there. I staid till bout 10 o'clock and came back to Camp. Time passed pleasantly, "on Angels' wings," while with Miss Mag.

Friday, 11th—Remained in camp.

Saturday, 12—I played off on an old Georgian as Captain or with Captain's uniform, got a buggy that a private could not have reached with a twenty foot pole. I and Oly Archer rode out in it to Mr. Ransom's. Took Mr. Jackson along with us. We took supper and sit til bedtime. Time passed delightfully. Pleasant drive back to camp.

Sunday, 13th—Moved eight miles from Rome out on the Kingston road to where the 4th Tennessee camped near a mill on the river.

Monday, 14th—Remained in camp all day.

Tuesday, 15th-Sunday, 20th—During this time I made the acquaintance of Miss Mary Reece, Miss Mary Davis and Miss Eugenie Holt. I spent all my leisure time visiting them. Very nice ladies indeed.

Monday, 21st—I and Mr. Nolin went up to the Tanyard this evening and took supper and sit till 10 o'clock. Miss E. was looking very nice indeed.

Tuesday—Reading My stories of Court of London.

Wednesday, 23rd—Reading Tempest and Sunshine. Went up to see Miss E. to-night. I spent a few hours at Mr. Davis; Miss Mollie and Cousin looking charming.

Thursday, 24th—Start this morning for Tunnel Hill. Came by T., left G.T. McGehee, got my boots $75. Bid Miss E. goodbye and in company with Capt. Hill and Wm. Nicholson came on eight miles and staid all night at Mr. Brownlee's.

Friday, 25th—Passed through Calhoun this morning, twenty-one miles to Dalton. Came on through D. to Tunnel Hill, seven miles from D.

Saturday, 26th—Came on to Ringgold and six miles beyond to Chickamauga. When we got in three miles of R. we struck the main Yankee line of invasion; from there on the country is destroyed—fencing burned, everything eat up and destroyed.

Sunday, 27th—We start up the railroad this morning but

turn back and camp on Chickamauga. Here we remain.

Monday 28th-October 1st, Thursday—Rain last night and still continuing; truly refreshing. First we've had for an age. All quiet in front. Well, I've missed being in one battle, that of Chickamauga.

October 2nd—Continued to rain all day.

3rd, Saturday—Moved camp this morning to Cherokee Springs one and one-half miles from Ringgold. Cousin Jimmy Hawkins met me and went to camp with me.

Sunday, 4th—I, Jim McGuire and Jimmy went out beyond Catoosa Springs and staid all night. A mistake. Saturday Eve.

Sunday, 4th—Took breakfast at Mr. Maston's this morning. Came by the Springs and stopped to see Miss Kate Shamblin. On to camp.

Monday, 5th—Remained in Camp.

Tuesday, 6th—I and Jimmy went out to the Springs; spent the night at Widow Conner's.

Wednesday, 7th—Piruted around generally. I left Jimmy at Mr. Smith's and went over to see Miss Kate.

Thursday, 8th—I came into Camp this morning, was appointed Adjutant of the Preps! Preps!

Friday, 9th—Jimmy came in this morning but did not stay long; was to be back in the evening.

Saturday, 10th—Jimmy did not come.

Sunday, 11th—I went out to see Miss Kate this morning, but heard nothing of Jim. Went by Mr. Shamblin's. Miss Eva and Miss Nannie were at home; two of the prettiest girls I've seen in Georgia. I went over to Mr. Smith's and heard of Jimmy; had gone on to Camp. I went back to Camp and found him there.

Monday, 12th—I went out this evening and staid all night with Mr. Cannon, at Mr. Smith's.

Tuesday, 13th—I started by daylight this morning and came to Camp. Raining.

Wednesday, 14th-Thursday, 15th—Nothing but rain, night and day.

Friday, 16th-Sunday, 18th—I went out to Catoosa Springs and to Mr. Shamblin's and back to Camp.

Monday, 19th-Wednesday, 21st.

Thursday, 22nd—This morning we start for Kingston. I came on in advance of the train to Tunnel Hill, saw all the boys and called around to see Miss Kate and Miss Nannie. They had moved down a few days ago. We came on four miles below Dalton and staid all night, I and Paul, Jim.

Friday, 23rd—Came on through to Calhoun and six miles below and staid all night. Raining all day and night.

Saturday, 24th—Came to Adairsville. Camp three miles from the village. To-night I went to Mr. Green's, one mile from A. with Wm. Campbell. Left my horse and went to town and took 10 o'clock train and went to Kingston. I staid but a few minutes; did not find what I went after. Came up at 12 o'clock to A., went out to Mr. Green's and staid all night.

Sunday, 25th—Went to town this morning and sent a letter to Tunnel Hill by Harper to Miss Nannie.

Monday, 26th-Wednesday, 28th—Nothing worthy of note.

Thursday, 29th—I went down to our old stamping ground to-day. I stopped to see Miss Eugenie Holt; had just returned from a visit to Marietta and was looking very pretty; stopped but a short time. Went on to Mr. Davis's; nobody at home but Miss Mollie. Crossed the River at Freeman's Ferry and went to Mr. Somers. Miss Maggie's husband at home. I staid all night. Miss Mattie came down this morning. I staid til bout 10 o'clock.

Friday, 30th—I came back to Mr. Davis; Mrs. D. and husband just starting to Rome. I took dinner and left. Came in to Mr. Green's, near Adairsville, and staid till bedtime and came to Camp.

Saturday, 31st—Remain in camp.

Sunday, 1st November—I went to town and mailed some letters, and out to Mr. Mooney's, the tanner, and got dinner; came by Mr. Green's, stopped awhile and on to Camp.

Monday, 2nd—Remain in Camp all day.

Tuesday, 3rd-Friday, 6th—Start this morning I and James Pickle down the country, stopped at Mr. Gillam's and took dinner. From there to Mr. Kit Dodd's and staid all night.

Saturday, 7th—I met Mr. Gore there, promised to write to Cousin Serena. Came on to Mr. Somer's and then to Van Wert; staid with Col. Jones to-night; met Mr. Jones and Lady, Mrs. Cullin and Miss Lou, daughter of the Colonel. Had a candy pulling.

Sunday, 8th—Came or went to Mr. Carmichael's and back to Van Wert before we found him. Jim left his leather with him and we came on to Capt. Wimberly's and staid all night.

Monday, 9th—Came in to Cedar Town this morning. Stay all night at the Hotel, ten dollars apiece. Sold some tobacco to him.

Tuesday, 10th—Came out with Clan Blakemore and Fuget to Mr. Thomas. I spent the night at John Hatchers. Miss Jane Simpson was there to-night. James Pickel was not with me; the other boys went back to town.

Wednesday, 11th—I spent the day and night at Mr. Hatchers.

Thursday, 12th—Went over to Mr. Thomas'. I made a girth for him. From there to Miss Kate Carter's. Mr. Shirry and two other gents came in, gentlemanly, merry.

Friday, 13th—I came over to Mr. Hatcher's.

Saturday, 14th—Left Mr. Hatcher's and came up to Cave Spring, saw Jenkins and Capt. Hooks. Mart Lee was there but I did not get to see him. Came on to Dr. Richardson's near Cedar Town and staid all night, a very fine family indeed. Has one grown daughter. Met Col. Bryant, a Kentucky refugee.

Sunday, 15th—Came on to Van Wert. Jim stopped at Carmichael's and got his boots. Came on to Mr. Peck's and to Mr. Somers; stopped and spent Monday.

November, 16th—Came this evening to Adairsville; found our Train gone to Charleston. Slept on the ground.

Tuesday, 17th—Went to Grandpaps this morning and got breakfast. Jim stopped at Mr. McDow's to see Reuben Stround. Came on and we started from Grandpaps. Came up to Mr. Curtis and turned off to the right. Came up to Silvacoa and camped; got corn from a field.

Wednesday, 18th—Got breakfast, paid two dollars for it and crossed the River. Came on to Spring Place, got heel plates put on. Came out seven miles and staid all night. Camped.

Thursday, 19th—Came on to-day to Charlestown and six miles above to Mr. Calloway's and staid all night.

Friday, 20th—Came on through Athens, Sweetwater and Philadelphia; came out one and one-half miles and took supper at a very nice place—Virginians. Met McMahon of Company H. I and Jim came on to Camp near London.

Saturday, 21st—Jim went to the Com. this morning. I had an offer for my mule this eve and sold him.

Sunday, 22nd—We remained in Camp.

Monday, 23rd—Moved Camp to within two miles of Lenoir on Little Tennessee River. I went out to Mr. Vassey's; let my clothing.

Tuesday, 24th—All quiet in Camp. Firing at Kingston, Wheeler and Wilder.

Wednesday, 25th-Thursday, 26th—Went to a dance to-night. I only danced two sets. Dr. Bob was with me. Came back about one o'clock.

Friday, 27th—Remained in Camp all day.

Saturday, 28th—Started this morning on a scout through Blunt—Charley Mason, John Kelison, Jessy Kirkland. Met up with Charley Pelham and Sam Piper.

Kirkendol of Company G was with us. Found Steve Gallagher and Jim with Mr. Upton. Jim was wounded; Steve came on with us. We crossed the River at Niles Ferry and staid all night at Mr. Norwood's.

Sunday, 29th—We went up the road two or three miles and found all the troopers leaving Blunt. We turned and came back to Mr. Norwood's and took dinner and came cross the River to Mr. Curtis and staid all night.

Monday, 30th—Charley Pelham came down this morning and told the Yanks were upon us and to fall back to Mr. Upton's. Kirk was pretty merry. Went down to Hawkins to get Sam Piper and Kirkland. We came up to Upton's, met Maj. Stevens, took dinner and sent after whiskey. Upton called up his negroes and gave them some whiskey and commenced the preparation for the move. I staid with them until they started. Four of us went to Cunningham's and staid all night.

Tuesday, 1st December—We came to Mr. White's this morning and there left Mr. Upton and started for the Telico Plains, I, Mason and Kelison. Met Kirkland, Piper and Kirkendol; then came up to McDermot's and staid all night.

Wednesday, 2nd—I and Kirk went to Cagle's and got his horses. I paid 200 to boot. Met at Mc D's. Four of us staid at Mr. Hunt's.

Thursday, 3rd—I came over to the shop and had my horse shod, and I and Kirk came on to Carmichael's. Found Pete Kendall there. The other Boys had gone. Met Bulger Peoples. Went on to Hawkins; found all the Boys there; staid all night.

Friday, 4th—Started for Motley Ford. Heard the Yanks were there and started for Carmichael's. Came on five or six miles and met up with Dick Tainter of Scott's Louisiana Regiment. Came on to C. and there divided; Sam Piper going to Mr. Shaw's with me and T. Had not been there long till the other boys came on. We got ready to start, and they refused and Sam piper [sic] with them. I and Tainter then left them and came on to Mr. Donohue's and staid all night. I have never taken such a pirute before nor never will again.

Saturday, 5th—Left Mr. Donohue's with Dick Tainter and came down to Mr. Carr's on the River, five miles above the mouth of Citico. Found them all gone up the River for North Carolina. Dick did not want to go to Blunt. We went across the River to Bright's and found several men, Briscow of Company K among them. We staid all night.

Sunday, 6th—We started for Holloway's with two of the Boys. We got there. Dick would go no further. Mint and Drew and Meroney all turned gack [back?]. I, Hugh Singleton and Briscow started for L. Came out to Old Major Pugh's and found the Yanks had prowled him of beehives and everything. Then came on cross Motley Ferry road and through a camp they had just left. Some Yankees on the ground laying up fences with the negroes. We came on cross Morgantown Road, found all the roads traveled by them. Came on to Capt. Dyer's, fed our horses and got supper and on to within one mile of Louisville. Stopped at Old Man Dyer's; found the Yanks in large force near him. Stopped, and fed and walked down to within three hundred yards of their camp fires. Could not get to the Planters Hotel. Came back; six of our boys were laying out in the woods near Mr. D's. We fed and slept in the barn till nearly day. Old Man woke us up, found two of the men were Carlton and Patton of Company F; others were Morgan Men. All came out to a thicket and spent the day.

Monday, 7th—Came in this evening to Mr. Dyer's, found the Yankees all gone, got supper and went down to the Planters, spent two or three hours. Gardner sold them a horse. I must take Miss Kate one. Came out to-night to Mr. Dyer's, warmed and came on to Lige Jim Henry's. I passed as a Yankee with Mrs. Henry. Came on to Mr. Holloway's and to Mr. Bess's and got dinner.

Tuesday, 8th—Came on to Mr. Bright's and staid all night; rained all day.

Wednesday, 9th—All quiet to-day. Didn't move.

Thursday, 10th—We start for Longstreet for or via Sevier. Gave it out and started for the vicinity of Bess' Mill. Went to see Mr. Jo Gray, a Lieut. in the Yankee Army. He was not at home; took two horses and a negro. Came on to McCully's and got two of them, two guns and one pistol, two horses. Came on to Bess' but found them all gone, then came gack [back?] to Mr. Bright's.

Friday, 11th—Started this evening for Sevier, got as far as Little River at Mr. McClane's and turn back. Two Yanks rode right through us. Came on by day near Mont Vale Spring. Stopped and got breakfast. Saw two Bushwhackers but could not catch them. Met Mr. King at the Springs. Came on over to Mr. Gomly's.

Saturday, 12th—I staid all night at Mr. Cutchberson's.

Sunday, 13th—All started to-night for Louisville. Rained and we separated; I, Smith and Alexander leaving the crowd at Mr. Everett's. We stopped at Mr. Best's and staid all night and all day.

Monday, 14th—Start to-night for Sevier; ran into the Yanks at Maryville; my saddle turned; I lost my horse. The Boys abandoned theirs and we made our escape on foot. Worked our way out to McClaine's on Little River just at daylight, but he would have nothing to do with us; could get no assistance from him. Came down the River and lay out in a little mot of timber.

Tuesday, 15th—Came to Hiram Bogle's, crossed the Little River at Finley's, the Sheriff of the County. Got to Bogle's and got a snack to eat. Mr. Bogle had taken the oath and would give me no information, only directions to Tim Chandler's.

Tuesday [Wednesday][*], *16th*—Came on to Chandler's, got lost on the road and had to stop and inquire at a house (John Robinson's). He told me about the Home Guards being in the neighborhood. I or we went on until we got to the house where they were camped or near it. The road forked and I went up to inquire about the road. Found 'twas not a dwelling and saw the Home Guards through the window. Went on to the next house, Mr. Johnson's, and got the information and traveled on. Got to C's 1 o'clock at night, found Mr. Houck there. Boys staid at the house while I went to the house. I took supper with them and got some meat and bread for the Boys. Miss Rogers was there. I could get but little information from Chandler. I went to the barn and we went into the straw to stay next day and cross at Bradson's next night.

Wednesday [Thursday], *17th*—This morning the Home Guards got on our tracks, and by the aid of Citizens found us and carried us back to the Academy. Randell is Capt., Cresivell first Lieut., Rose 2nd, Moore a Private, Ingle, Keener and others.

Thursday [Friday], *18th*—Start this morning for Knoxville; get in bout 1 p.m. Capt. Barnetts takes charge of me and sends me to Prison.

Friday [Saturday], *19th*—I find one of the 11th Texas here, three or four of the 2nd Georgia. I send out a summons to the Lodge for asistance; two members call on me and promise to attend to my case, but I hear no more from them. Another squad of 96 prisoners came in. also three of Morgans men, Messrs. Church and Smith.

Maj. Smith of Wheeler's staff called on us. Two other squads came in. With the last came Will Morton of the

---

*There is confusion of days and dates from "Tuesday, 16th" to "Thursday,25," for the 16th is Wednesday, the 17th is Thursday, etc.

Battery or Company F. Alexander takes the oath and left us. Morton, myself, the two Churches and two Smiths form the mess.

Sunday [Monday], *21st*—Parson ... preached for us this evening.

Thursday [Friday], *25th*—A dull Christmas. Receiving one-quarter pound bread a day and bout one pound beef, no wood hardly—freezing and starving by inches. All this brings me up to the 29th Monday [Tuesday]. Morton tried to get to see his sister but could not. The Parson came in and informed him that she died at 3 o'clock this morning. Such is the fate of war. In 150 yards of her and yet could not get to see her.

Wednesday, 30th—Morton out on street parole.

Thursday, 31st—Miss Anna Brooks came around, Miss McMullin with her, brought me a pair of socks. I sent a note to Mrs. House by Hupplits to-night.

Friday, 1st day of January, 1864—Received one pair of drawers from Miss Nannie Scott, two shirts from Mrs. House. One hundred and fifty of the prisoners start to-day for Strawberry Plains. We go to-morrow.

———

Dodd was sentenced to death on or before January 5th. An extract from a letter by the general commanding and dated at Knoxville, Tenn., January 17, 1864, reads:

"I also avail myself of this opportunity to forward an order publishing the proceedings, findings and sentence in the case of Private E.S. Dodd, Eighth Texas Confederate Cavalry, who was tried, condemned and executed as a spy.

"I also inclose a copy of an order which I have found it necessary to issue, in regard to the wearing of the U.S. uniform by Confederate soldiers."

"Inclosure No. 7 (here omitted) contains General Orders, No. 3, Department of the Ohio, January 5, 1864, promulgating charges, findings and sentence to death in the case of E.S. Dodd, Eighth Texas Cavalry, arrested and tried as a spy."

—*War of the Rebellion*, Series III, Vol. 4. p. 53.

Hanging As A Spy
by
Robert F. Bunting

The circumstances of Dodd's conviction as a spy and his agonizing death were told vividly by Robert F. Bunting, Chaplain of the Terry Texas Rangers, in a letter to the Houston Daily Telegraph published in the issue of April 13, 1864. Even though 132 years have passed, it is not easy to read Bunting's account without feeling remorse over Dodd's death. Had he been killed suddenly in battle, Dodd would have been one of the many unfortunate and long forgotten victims of the war; but the slow, premeditated and "legalized" killing by his captors made his death a tragedy and one not easily forgotten. As rugged as they were, the Rangers undoubtedly repaid the Federals many times over for hanging Dodd.

—Tom Munnerlyn
Austin, Texas
May, 1996

It is a proud reflection for an old Ranger to look around and see so many of his comrades promoted to positions of honor, trust and usefulness. But with all our success, there is now and then a painful circumstance which throws a melancholy sadness over all our spirits and clouds our joy. The death of E.S. Dodd, Co. D, who was hung in Knoxville on the 8th day of January, under the charge of being a spy, brings to the heart more bitterness than any calamity which has overtaken us.

He was captured about the 17th of December in Sevier county, some eighteen miles from Knoxville. He was brought to that city and confined in the county jail in which Confederate prisoners are kept. It seems that he lost his horse in the Middle Tennessee raid, and, unwilling to remain in the wagon camp, he had followed us into East Tennessee, and, getting a horse, he was making his way through the lines of the enemy; for we had fallen back, leaving him in his lines.

It appears that during his confinement, it occurred to the authorities that charges might be preferred against him, and a court martial could convict him. It seems there was a gallows on which one or more bridge-burners, during our possession of East Tennessee, had been hung by the civil law, and it was the expressed desire of Brownlow and others of his kind, that some rebel should die upon the same spot. Here was a Texas Ranger in their power, and it would be double gratification of fiendish delight to execute him, but they must have the semblance of martial law to cover up the infamous deed.

In the first place Mr. Dodd wore the blue pants and overcoat which Gens. Rosecrans and Burnside had declared an offence punishable by death. Then on his person was found a private diary, in which were noted two points—1st, he mentioned having passed himself for a Yankee; and 2nd, that he had gained all necessary information with reference to the enemy's pickets. In regard to the clothing, he plead that he had worn them from necessity, and not from choice, which is true, not only in the case of Mr. Dodd, but with many others in our army; for the Yankee quartermasters furnish us with the most of our clothing. In reference to the items in his diary, he plead that, as to the first, he was accidentally inside of their lines and among a Union population, and he passed himself off for a Union soldier in order to get lodging and provisions and to avoid detection; then, as to the second, he was working his way through their lines, and his inquiries were in reference to the pickets in order that he might avoid them and escape capture. But no explanations, denials or protestations were of any avail: he was the selected victim, and judgment was to go against him.

Accordingly, as he declared to those with whom he conversed, without anything like a fair trial, he was convicted of being a spy, and sentenced to be hung on Friday, the 8th day of January. As an evidence of his innocence of the charge, he wore when captured and to the hour of his death, his Mexican blanket, his sombrero and Texas star (I believe he always wore on his hat the printed star, with "Terry's Texas Rangers" around it, together with a small silver star, which is recognized through both armies as the badge of a Texas Ranger) which are singular marks for a rebel spy to wear within the enemy's lines.

In the letters which he left—directed to his father in Kentucky, to his grandfather in Mississippi, to Mr. Maxwell, near Austin, Texas, and others—he gave an account of his trial and condemnation, the visits of ministers to him in his cell, and sent messages of love to the parties addressed, and, in view of his execution, declared that "he was as innocent of the charge of being a spy as an angel of light." The three Federal chaplains, and Rev. Joseph H. Martin, pastor of a Presbyterian church in Knoxville, since sent through our lines, all believed him innocent. The guards who were with him were of the same opinion.

Mr. Dodd was a "bright Mason," a worthy and efficient member of the "Terry Lodge" connected with our regiment, and, as was his privelege [sic], he sent word to the Masonic fraternity in the city, and was visited by several of them. As Masons they believed him innocent, and some of the Federal officers who belonged to the order, were so thoroughly convinced of his innocence, that they applied to the commanding general for clemency in behalf of the prisoner; but he replied, in substance, that he had been tried and found guilty by a court martial, and therefore the sentence must be executed.

Accordingly, on the appointed day, shortly after ten o'clock, Ephraim Smith Dodd was taken from the prison, and led away to the place which was to be the scene of his slow and fiendish murder. He met his fate like a hero: there was not a muscle moved, nor an indication of fear. At 11 o'clock, the drop fell, but the rope, which was slender, broke, and his body fell upon the ground. The shock was very severe, but not sufficiently to render him unconscious, for after falling to the ground, he was heard to say, "release me if you please." At once the crowd of unfeeling soldiery gathered around him, and after rolling and rubbing him for fifteen minutes, he had sufficiently revived to again walk up upon the scaffold, his head meanwhile rolling in agony, and with some assistance to stand up until the rope was adjusted to his neck, and the second time, the drop fell and at half past 11 o'clock, the gallant Ranger was pronounced dead!

His body was taken down and removed to a burying ground immediately north of Gray Cemetery and there it was deposited with its mother earth. A friend followed his remains to the grave and directed that his name be put on the headboard for future identity.

Thus a cultivated, honorable gentleman, a true friend, a sincere christian [sic], a "bright Mason," a faithful and brave soldier, has been murdered—publicly murdered in cold blood. His record is preserved and in due time it will be produced. The letters were handed over to the Federal Chaplain, but will doubtless be suppressed by the military, for they were the plain utterances of an honest man and an honest soldier of the Confederacy.

Rome, Georgia
March 4th, 1864

INDEX

Names in parentheses, following the names as mentioned by Giles, Blackburn and Dodd, are the names as listed in the Compiled Service Records of Confederate Soldiers who served in Organizations From the State of Texas (National Archives, Washington, D.C.) and/or the names as listed by John M. Claiborne for the reunion of The Terry's Texas Rangers in 1882. In some cases, only the most similar names that can be identified are listed within the parentheses.

Illustration credits:

Archives Division, Texas State Library: *plates* 1, 12, 17, 29

Batchelor-Turner Letters 1861-1864. Annotated by H.J.H. Rugeley: *plates* 13, 14

Battle Flags of Texans in the Confederacy by Alan K. Sumrall: *plates* 3, 9

Battles and Leaders of the Civil War. Edited by R.U. Johnson & C.C. Buel: *plate* 10

Confederate Military History. Vol. XI. Edited by C.A. Evans: *plate* 6

Ollie Ray (Webb) Edwards: *plate* 26

The Encyclopedia of the New West. Edited by John Henry Brown: *plate* 20

The Life of Albert Sidney Johnston. By William Preston Johnston: *plate* 5

The Life Record of Henry W. Graber, A Terry Texas Ranger. By H.W. Graber: *plate* 8

Historical Review of South-East Texas. Edited by D.H. Hardy: *plates* 21, 22, 24

A History of Central and Western Texas. Edited by B.B. Paddock: *plate* 16

A History of Texas and Texans. By Frank W. Johnson: *plate* 23

A Memorial and Biographical History of McLennan, Falls, Bell and Coryell Counties, Texas: *plates* 7, 15, 19

Personnel of the Texas State Government. By L.E. Daniell: *plates* 25, 27, 28

Six Decades in Texas or Memoirs of Francis Richard Lubbock. Edited by C.W. Raines: *plate* 4

State House Press photo file: *plate* 18

Terry's Texas Rangers [Pemberton Press Reprint]. By L.B. Giles: *plate* 2

Texas in the War 1861-1865. Compiled by M.J. Wright, edited by H.B. Simpson: *plate* 11